P

"This is a very thought-provoking collection. It is useful to read for inspiration or devotional discussion. I found sample chapters very interesting and was attracted to other titles, in particular: 'What I Asked For,' 'Characteristics of One Who is Growing,' 'The Unfulfilled Dream,' and 'Thoughts of a Soldier at Christmas.'"

—Charles R. Miner (Bob)

Major, US Air Force

Retired

"Herb is a man who lives simply and loves deeply. Though the objects of his love are multi-faceted (God, family, country, military service, and life itself) the unifying factor of his work is a sense of gratitude that bleeds through each essay. Those who are drawn to living a life with gratitude will find Herb's work much to think about."

—Eric Mc Glade, Pastor

Trinity United Methodist Church

Bowling Green, Ohio

raise for Others

others

others

Christian and Patriotic Inspirational
Verses, Poems, and Prayers

Collected by
Herbert Dettmer

TATE PUBLISHING
AND **ENTERPRISES**, LLC

Published by Tate Publishing & Enterprises, LLC
127 E. Trade Center Terrace | Mustang, Oklahoma 73064 USA
1.888.361.9473 | www.tatepublishing.com

Tate Publishing is committed to excellence in the publishing industry. The company reflects the philosophy established by the founders, based on Psalm 68:11,
"The Lord gave the word and great was the company of those who published it."

Book design copyright © 2012 by Tate Publishing, LLC. All rights reserved.
Cover design by Kate Stearman
Interior design by Blake Brasor

Published in the United States of America

ISBN: 978-1-61862-640-0
1. Religion, Christian Life, Inspirational
12.3.12

Dedication

Herbert Dwight Fish
(1922-1945)
Staff Sergeant, US Army

Herbert Dwight Fish was a quiet, peace-loving young man. A college student in 1940, who thought war and violence were wrong, he was also, as many people of his generation were, a true "die-hard" American. When Pearl Harbor was attacked, he felt it was his duty and responsibility to stand up and defend our country, even though war was abhorrent to him. He enlisted in the army and soon was sent to the Pacific Theater. Keep in mind this was 1941 and the start of World War II, not Vietnam, the Persian Gulf War, or the War on Terrorism.

Herbert Fish died before I was born, yet I have been inspired by his life and his commitments. As a child I was told I was given his name and he gave his life fighting for our nation and our freedom. I didn't understand the meaning of this then. As I matured, I slowly realized just how committed he was. He was committed to serving God as well as his country. As an infantryman he knew the dangers he faced. As a man of faith he knew he could also serve God.

Herbert wrote and collected many verses, poems, and prayers before and during the war. These and others were used in various prayer and fellowship groups he led and attended. This collection includes many of his writings. Staff Sergeant Herbert Fish was awarded the Bronze Star with *V* for valor and the Purple Heart for his actions in combat in November 1944. While leading his men into battle on April 21, 1945, on the island of Okinawa, he gave his life. "Greater love has no man than this, that he lay down his life for his friends," (John 15:13).

Herbert served God by inspiring his men, leading them in battle and in prayer. His dedication to our faith and our freedom has earned my deepest admiration and respect.

Herbert Fish loved his friends, his country, and his God. He gave his life for what he loved. This collection, which was inspired by his service and his writings, is dedicated to his memory, so all may share his wisdom, his inspiration, and his love. Had he lived, he was going to enter the Christian ministry to continue his service to *others*.

—hd

Acknowledgements

Any project or undertaking needs the love and support of those close to you. "Others" has been a project that has taken several years of reading, collecting, writing rewriting and editing. This could not have been done without love and support of my wife Becky, my daughter Katie, my son Andy and my mother-in-law Bonnie. Their encouragement and their understanding of my work are beyond measure. Thank You!

To all the staff at Tate Publishing, in guiding me through the publishing process and answering my, probably too numerous, questions, I say, Thank You, for a job well done.

This has been a joy to do, as well as a very enlightening and humbling experience.

—Herb Dettmer, February, 2012

Table of Contents

Foreword

The purpose of this collection is to encourage the reader to think about what life is really all about. Thinking, acting, and living as He intended and taught us is the only way to true happiness. While I'm not a theologian or biblical scholar, I am a Christian and an American.

The reason I have included both religious verses and patriotic prose in this collection is to remind us, even though we have religious freedom in our country and *every* belief and faith is accepted and respected, the United States is *primarily* a Christian nation. There is no intent to slight any religious belief. As a Christian and an American, I feel it is important to include both secular and religious thought in this collection.

Except for the first two entries, "Others" and "Genesis 1:1," there is no special order in which these verses appear. I'd like to thank those unknown people whose writings are part of this collection. None of the material used in "Others" is, to the best of my knowledge, copyrighted except as noted. Being in the public domain, I freely use them. Every effort has been made to give proper credit to the authors of the various verses.

Biblical verses, as noted, were taken from the King James Version of the Holy Bible, copyright 1964 by Heirloom Bible Publishers; copyright 1971 by Devore & Sons, Inc.; The Standard American Edition of the Revised Version of the Bible, copyright 1901, by Thomas Nelson & Sons; copyright 1929 by

International Council of Religious Education. The latter Bible is the one Herbert Fish took overseas. It was given to me by his mother.

—hd

Preface

Since ancient times, the human race has been inspired by the thoughts of others. These thoughts, at first, were merely spoken, passed down through the generations, and remembered. Later, as written languages developed, these were put in a more permanent form. High priests, prophets, political leaders, and even average men and women—especially average men and women—have recited and written poems, prayers, and verses. These have been repeated from one generation to the next over the millennia.

This collection is my humble contribution to this ancient tradition. Included are numerous well-known poems and verses, as well as some previously published material. Some of the unpublished work was written or collected by Herbert D. Fish, the only child of very close family friends who was killed in World War II. When I was born, I was given his name, demonstrating the close ties of our two families. I was given his personal papers and Bible by his mother shortly before her death. Over the years, I have accumulated other verses and decided to share them in published form.

The comments following these verses, poems, and prayers were written by me and are solely my feelings, opinions, and beliefs. I have identified the source of each entry, although some are unknown or anonymous. I've included thoughts and questions at the end of my comments to assist in group discussions and to encour-

age the reader to contemplate his or her own feel-
ings and beliefs. When reading the section about the
months, think about some special event or occasion, in
addition to birthdays and anniversaries.

—hd

Contributors

Herbert D. Fish. See dedication page.

Edith Podreskey. Edith, or "The Rose Lady," was the grandmother of my wife, Rebecca. She wrote numerous verses and poems as well raising roses. A devoted wife, mother, grandmother, great-grandmother, and dear friend to all who knew her, she is truly missed.

Bonnie J. O'Brien. Bonnie, my mother-in-law, continued the family tradition of writing verses and poems.

Rebecca Dettmer. Wife, mother, grandmother— Rebecca continues following in her family's footsteps, writing as time allows in her busy schedule.

Herbert Dettmer. Husband, father, grandfather, part-time writer, and columnist for local newspaper, he is retired from the printing industry and is a US Army veteran.

Others

Lord, help me live from day to day,
in such a self-forgetful way,
that even when I kneel to pray,
my prayers will be for Others.

Help me in all the work I do,
to ever be sincere and true,
and know that all I do for you,
must be done for Others.

Others, Lord, yes Others,
let this my motto be,
help me live for Others,
that I may live like Thee.

Source: H. D. Fish

In every aspect of life throughout history, there can be two types of people found: leaders and followers. It's true in religion, business, industry, education, government, and any other area. Every religion has its clergy, the trained spiritual leaders who convey the word of God, Jehovah, Allah, or whatever name they give the Creator, to the believers—the followers.

Every business enterprise is owned by investors, as few as one to hundreds or perhaps thousands of stock-holders. These investors directly or indirectly hire the executives, managers, and workers to run the business and produce the product or service for its customers. The various educational systems have teachers and students. It doesn't matter if the system is an advanced college or university or Mom or Dad teaching their child to ride a bike. Government is the same way, from pre-historic clans and tribes to the contemporary national governments of today where there are presidents, prime ministers, kings, chiefs, and other titles and the citizens—the taxpayers or subjects, also known as followers. Everyone has a part in whatever society or country in which they live. The leaders teach, give guidance (or orders), while the followers offer their services and support. All have important jobs, and all are dependent in some way on *others*.

If we could think less about ourselves and more about other people, how much better the world would be? Think how much cleaner our environment would be. Think how peace would be more prevalent than war. Instead of praying for our own wants, needs, and desires, maybe we should pray more for the wants, needs, and desires of *others*—just like the golden rule says, just like Jesus taught us. Not that we should forget about ourselves and our families.

In our church work we should determine *why* we are doing our part. Is it so we feel better about ourselves? Is it so we get our name printed in the church bulletin or newsletter so everyone knows what we are doing and how "wonderful" we are? Or are we *truly* trying to help *others*? Do we want to help those in need? If that is the reason, then why do we need the ego gratification of publicity? Live, act, and do for *others*—those in need, even those not in need—"that we may live like Thee."

—hd

Can we live as Christians in this mindless, selfish, "I *deserve* it all" world and still follow the Golden Rule?

Genesis 1:1

"In the beginning, God…"

Genesis 1:1

Source: H. D. Fish's personal Bible

Depending on to whom you talk, God is either our heavenly Father or Mother, our Creator, Sovereign, Lord, or any of the numerous other "politically correct" names that have been used in recent years. Does it matter *what* we call God? That too depends on to whom you talk. Some say God is divine, holy, sacred, and on and on. Others may say it doesn't matter as long as we believe, follow His Ten Commandments, and are reverent.

Does it or doesn't? To the average man, woman, and child, it may matter more *how* or *if* we practice our beliefs and obey God's laws. Biblical scholars, theologians, and church bureaucrats can debate, discuss, study, and argue all they want, but the average person who sits in the pew on Sunday morning could care less about the intellectual debate. All he or she wants is to hear the Word of God—to worship, pray, and take part in the sacraments.

To answer the question of who or what is God, let's look at Genesis 1: "In the beginning, God created the heavens and the earth." What about before the "beginning"? What existed? Was there anything? *No!* No heavens, no earth, no sun, no other planets, and no stars. Nothing. Only God. So one day, God decided—wait a minute—if there were no stars or sun, there was no light. No light, no day, or night, just a void of emptiness. Whatever force, person, or thing God is, if there was anything in existence before the beginning, God alone knows. Anyway, God decided to create, out of this void of emptiness, the heavens—meaning the universe—and the earth. Now, how can something be created out of nothing? Any school child who has taken basic science has learned that matter cannot be created or destroyed but merely changed from one form to another. So how could God create the heavens and the earth out of a void of emptiness? Obviously God never went to school. How could He? (She? It?) Before the earth was created, there were no schools, only an empty void—and God. (Maybe this is a clue about the magnitude of God's ultimate supremacy).

Instead of trying to label or name God, as our mother or father or something else, we should just accept God as *the* all-powerful force of whatever we can see and read about. Before anything, before time, God existed. We must accept this on faith. There is no way man or woman or science can prove otherwise. All we have is the Holy Bible that tells us, "In the beginning, God…" Out of nothing, God created everything. From the pesky mosquito that bothers us in the summer and the cat's or dog's fleas, to the giant sequoia, the mountains, and the vast oceans. God created the pleasant and gentle warm summer breezes as well as the destructive force of hurricanes, earthquakes, and volcanoes.

In the beginning there was only God. God, our heavenly Father, our creator, created everything, then created us—man and woman. Who are we to question who or what God is? Shouldn't we just accept the fact that "In the beginning" there was God?

—hd

Just *who* or *what* is God?

God's Garden

At the end of the day,
as I sit in deep meditation
in this garden of God's own creation,
another day has done its best
and the setting sun has gone to rest.
The shadows have long since passed away.
It's the end of another day.

Soft little breezes begin their dance,
and the cool evening dew caresses the plants.
Knowing I have done my best
gives me peace of mind while I sit and rest.
As in the garden silence now reposes,
and the day at last is gone,
I drink in the fragrance of the roses
and say a prayer to God's own Son.

Source: Edith Podresky

It's summer, and the day fades into evening. The sun slowly sets. Shadows lengthen then merge together as the day ends and night begins. The quiet evening coolness offers a peace not possible during the day.

In our busy, hectic world, night still follows day, giving us the opportunity to slow down and rest. The animal world rests, as does the plant world. Instead of living the constant pressure-filled lives we are used to, inviting such problems as heart attacks, strokes, and high blood pressure, we would be wise to follow the examples of the animal and plant kingdoms.

Soft breezes dance in the darkened world of night, and dew coats the plants. As one would sit quietly, relaxing, enjoying the peaceful garden, thinking, remembering the hot sting of the afternoon sun. The garden is at rest. The soft, moist soil and the sweet fragrance of the roses tantalize the senses. All is well. The day's work is done. The garden, the plants, even the bees are all at rest as we should be. Evening, night, the time for peaceful reflection on the day just passed, the time for solitude, for quiet. Another day is gone. What is done is done. What wasn't done can't be done, not now, not today. We can't go back and relive the day just ended. We can't redo whatever good we did, nor can we undo what we shouldn't have done. All we can do now is remember, reflect, and learn from our deeds and our misdeeds. Remember, learn, and pray for guidance and forgiveness.

Remembering, we just work the soil and tend the flowers. It's not really our garden, but God's, just as our lives are not really our own. God gave us life and a mind to reason with—to learn, to follow His Commandments, and His Son's teachings.

A prayer in the quiet coolness of the evening, what better way to end the day?

—hd

Are there other gardens (besides the one in the back-yard) that we need to work, weed, and tend the soil?

Letting Go

To let go doesn't mean to stop caring;

   it means I can't do it for someone else.

To let go is not to cut myself off;

   it is the realization that I can't control another.

To let go is not to enable;

   but to allow learning from natural
   consequences.

To let go is to admit powerlessness;

   which means the outcome is not in my hands.

To let go is not to try to change or blame
another;

   I can only change myself.

To let go is not to care for,

   but to care about.

To let go is not to fix,

   but to be supportive.

To let go is not to judge,

   but to allow another to be a human being.

To let go is not to try to arrange all the outcomes,

   but to allow others to effect their outcomes.

To let go is not to be protective;

   it is to permit another to face reality.

To let go is not to deny,
> but to accept.

To let go is not to nag, scold, or argue,
> but to search out my own shortcomings and correct them.

To let go is not to adjust everything to my desires, but to take each day as it comes, and cherish the moment.

To let go is not to criticize or regulate anyone,
> but to try to become whatever dream I can be.

To let go is to know life isn't about me,
> but rather it's about others.

To let go is not to regret the past,
> but to grow and live for the future.

To let go is to fear less
> and to love more.

Source: Unknown

In a world of money, success, "gotta have it all," and "gotta be the best," our society has become selfish and uncaring. Everyone it seems is only concerned about what is best for them. "What's in it for me?" seems to be the prevailing attitude. We feel the need to be in control of everything, even if it means alienating those around us.

Yet, in times of crisis or tragedy, like the attacks on September 11, the Christmas tsunami, hurricanes Katrina and Rita, the Haiti earthquake, and the earthquake and tsunami in Japan, we realize there is more to life than our selfishness.

We are all living on God's earth together. Whatever we do, in some way or other, is going to affect someone else, whether it is a positive or a negative deed. Letting go is not ignoring a problem or situation but rather allowing everyone the chance to be themselves. By giving hope, guidance, support, and love, people will learn to take care of their lives.

Everyone may need help on occasion. Help is given, or at least offered. But God gave all of us a will to survive. It is our duty—our responsibility—to do that however we can while following God's laws and Ten Commandments.

—hd

How do we show we care about others without taking away their self-respect?

The Serenity Prayer

God, grant me the serenity to accept the things
I cannot change,
The courage to change the things I can,
And the wisdom to know the difference.

Source: Unknown

Today's world being an intense, complex, and competitive environment offers many opportunities—many choices. Opportunities for personal and career advancement and educational opportunities are numerous. With modern technology advancing our standard of living almost daily, there seems to be little time to do more than just try to keep up with all these advances and improvements. We must keep up, or we'll lose any chance to catch up later. Is it any wonder that our society has seen a dramatic increase in stress-related medical problems such as high blood pressure, strokes, and heart attacks?

Computers, fax machines, modems, cell phones, the Internet, laser this and laser that, fiber optics, and so many more have invaded and virtually taken over the workplace, our homes, our recreational time, and even our churches. No matter where we go or what we do, technology gets us there, helps us do whatever, and returns us to where we started. Our schedules are full at work, at home, at church, in our community service, and even in our recreational time. We need to schedule, prioritize, and adjust. Most of us carry cell phones so we can always be in touch with whoever may need us. At a family picnic, at church, even on the golf course, and in the bowling alley, someone's cell phone often can be heard.

Serenity? What serenity? "I don't have time," or, "We're so busy, we can't." How often have we heard either of these comments? How many times have each of us uttered one of these? Serenity? Who has time for it? We're either working, playing, or socializing, all of which can be stressful. Serenity? Is there any in our modern society? There must be. There has to be somewhere, someplace, some time to *stop, stop* to unwind, to relax without interruption, without concern. Are we missing something important? There must be a way to escape our cell phone.

We prioritize and adjust our schedules for leisure time and "quiet time." Yet we still feel the need to keep going and doing until one day the heart says enough, or maybe the brain says it. Heart attacks and strokes plague men and women of all backgrounds and heritages. The next time we stop to prioritize, maybe we should just *stop* and find the courage to change what we can. Change our lives. We could change jobs or occupations, but that doesn't always get us out of the rat race. We still need to support ourselves and our families. Try as we do to spend that extra hour with loved ones, or an extra day, the lawn still needs to be mowed, the car washed, and our kids bike needs to be fixed—*now!*

Finding courage to change what we can isn't easy. The demands that are made on us are great. We may want to change, but we need help. And help is as hard to find as courage. Or is it? Real help is just a prayer away. God is always there, all we need to do is ask. Ask God for the courage and help we need to make the changes we know we should make, could make, and want to make. There are many things we can change, and with His help we can. There are many, perhaps even more, things we cannot change—the boss's mind on what we feel is a critical problem, our spouse's desire to redo the living room, our children's friends, the weather, the tax laws, or our neighbor's attitude.

There is one thing we can change, however: our attitude. With God's help we can do that. With God's help we can accept the things we cannot change, and with God's help we will have "the wisdom to know the difference."

—hd

Do we have time for "quiet" time? Do we really need "quiet" time?

Once Again—Christmas

Like a blanket of softly falling snow,
the gentle Spirit of Christmas covers the world.

Once again, our thoughts reach out toward the
star of higher things.
Once again, a child will lead us.

Once again, a babe is King.
Once again, Faith, Hope and Love are abroad
in the land.

Crisis, earthquake, flood, and storm,
tornado, riot, and war cannot destroy it.

Once again, good news conquers evil.
The darkness of fear cannot blot out its light.

Hatred, envy, and jealousy retreat from it.
Nothing can stop its onward march into the
hearts of men.

The Spirit of *Christmas* lives!

Source: Edith Podresky

Written for the mid-week Call to Worship,
December 13, 1974,
First United Methodist Church,
Valparaiso, Indiana

Used with permission

As the soft, pure, white snow covers the land, the Spirit of Christmas descends upon us once again. As three men bearing gifts, long ago, traveled to a humble stable, we travel today, bearing the fruits of our labor. The three men followed a bright, shining star, brighter than any they had ever seen. Knowing it must be of some great importance, they followed it until it led them to the infant. Did they know who this baby was? Were they told, as the shepherds were, of the importance of this birth in a humble stable? Did they understand? Or was it their faith and wisdom that told them?

That first Christmas brought faith, hope, and love to the world. God's gift of His only Son taught us the *Spirit* of giving. The three travelers presented their gifts in that spirit, as we do today and have throughout history. The *Spirit* moves us and guides us to offer our gifts.

The Spirit lives! During man-made or natural disasters people give willingly, lovingly, and eagerly of their time, money, and resources to those in need. The

Spirit lives, as good conquers bad, love conquers hate, as light conquers dark just as the soft, pure, white snow covers the land.

The Spirit lives, and nothing can stop it or kill it—not disasters, not negative emotions. No legislative body can regulate or ban it. (Some have tried but without success.) Not even the passage of time can stop or destroy the Spirit of Christmas.

Often the Spirit has been tested. Many governments have tried to destroy it, yet the Spirit lives! It cannot be seen, though it is all around us like a blanket of snow. It cannot be touched, yet it touches us all. It makes not a sound but can be heard all around the world—from the smallest gift, like holding the door for someone or comforting a friend, to the greatest gift of all, the birth of our Savior.

The Spirit of giving—of Christmas—lives!

—hd

What else can give us the Spirit of Christmas?

A Cross and a Crown

When the time does come
For us to lay our burdens down,
We'll be glad that we have lost the cross–
And that we have gained the crown.

Source: Edith Podresky

When Christ carried the burdensome cross to Calvary, was it just part of the crucifixion? Or was it symbolic of His carrying the sins of the world?

Throughout our lives we carry various burdens. As young children, just growing up can be a burden. As adolescents, maturing physically and emotionally can be a burden so great that many teens find it very difficult to cope with it. Striving hard to be grown-ups, they are often afraid to let go of their childhood. Young adults, finally grown up, are quickly hit with the burdens of reality in the real world. During the rest of our lives, burdens of increasing responsibilities weigh heavily on our shoulders. Jobs and careers, spouses, children, community activities, and planning and preparing for retirement can burden us with too much to do in too little time. Responsibility may give us authority, which leads to power. The burden of power has ruined many political leaders, many business leaders, and many other people in positions of influence. Just take a look at nearly any news story, and there will be some reference to fraud, corruption, or lack of good judgment.

How we manage these many burdens of life, whether the burdens are positive or negative, is a true measure of our success. Too many times we measure our success in terms of position, material goods, and power, as if success can be bought or otherwise obtained, a tangible goal. The Judge Supreme has the only set of standards that count. Whatever standards of measurement we use are immaterial and meaningless. What we do to impress our friends and associates won't matter on judgment day. What does matter is how we carry our burdens and manage our lives. God has given each of us various burdens to carry. God has also given each of us the rulebook to guide us as we carry these burdens. God has even given us a Savior to help.

Christ carried the burdens of the world to Calvary. He has His crown; we know that. When our time comes to lay aside our earthly burdens, will we have gained *our* crown?

—hd

Just how many crosses do have to bear? What is the significance of them? Is there a purpose for them?

Symbols and Creatures

Throughout our world we can find many different symbols. Nations, religions, organizations, businesses, ethnic groups, and sports teams all have certain symbols that identify each group. Some of these symbols are official or traditional, while others are well recognized or just accepted. Many, perhaps most, have some special significance.

The star of Bethlehem and cross at Calvary hold a special meaning to Christians, the menorah and Star of David are equally important to the Jewish people. The maple leaf and Mounties of Canada, the pyramids of Egypt, the Russian bear, and the fleur di leis are but a few national symbols well known worldwide.

The bald eagle with its majestic appearance both in flight and sitting on a tree branch is one more national symbol recognized throughout the world. The symbol of the United States of America has inspired generations of Americans to strength, fortitude, and independence.

The oyster, though a valuable part of the commercial fishing industry and a source of natural and cultured pearls for jewelry, hardly is inspirational or the subject of paintings, figurines, and calendars. While it is a delicacy in some areas of our nation and the world, many people have never even seen one.

God created all creatures that live on our earth, each one having special and unique characteristics. Each one He gave a purpose. Those like the oyster, made passive and virtually defenseless, God protects and cares for. The oyster was given a hard shell to protect itself and an easy way to nourish itself.

But to those creatures like the bald eagle, who God made strong, majestic, and powerful, He gave the world. With strength, intellect, and the desire to "make it on their own," the bald eagle chooses to live up high in the rugged mountains, safe from what few enemies it has. For nourishment, the eagle flies for miles in all kinds of weather, free and confident. The eagle is strong, independent, and free, limited only by its abilities and the clear blue skies, just like the American people—strong, independent, and free. Not passive and defenseless like the oyster.

The eagle, the majestic eagle, not the oyster, was chosen long ago as the symbol for the United States of America.

Source: Herbert Dettmer

What other symbols do we have to represent our faith? Our country?

The Pledge of Allegiance

I pledge allegiance to the flag
of the United States of America,
and to the republic for which it stands,
One nation, under God, indivisible,
with liberty and justice for all.

Source: Originally published in 1892, in a
magazine, "Youth's Companion," written by
Frances Bellamy

How many times have we recited the "Pledge of Allegiance?" How many times have we thought about what it really means? Have we *ever really* thought about what the words we repeat mean?

I pledge...

I promise on my honor and my life. What more can a person do when making a pledge or promise? What is more important and valuable than one's own life and honor? Our founding fathers swore allegiance to the cause of freedom on their lives, their fortunes, and their sacred honor. Before our society became so complex, one's honor meant everything. Even sworn enemies fought honorably and treated each other with respect. When we pledge, we are making a solemn vow, a promise, an obligation.

Allegiance...

Is a faithfulness, loyalty, or fidelity to whatever we hold dear. Faithfulness, loyalty, and fidelity—strong, powerful words for strong, powerful feelings. A nation's flag, flown high, is a visible statement to anyone who sees it. The area over which it flies is that country's territory. It is a visible statement that the viewer is in that particular nation. Our flag, the stars and stripes, flies over the United States of America.

To the flag of the United States of America...

The flag of our nation has been held high, saluted, respected, and honored. We all know what it looks like. But do we know how many Americans have fought for it? Fought for the privilege of defending it against its enemies? Do we know how many have died defending it? Fought and died for the freedoms it stands for? From the red stripes, which represent the blood spilled defending it, to the white stripes, which represent the purity of the principle of freedom, to the white stars, which represent all the states, to the blue field, which represents the sky over our beloved country, "from sea to shining sea." A country that despite its problems is still sought after by oppressed people, people who risk their lives to escape their homelands for the freedoms and opportunities we too often take for granted.

And to the Republic for which it stands...

How many of us know we do not live in a democracy? At least according to the "Pledge of Allegiance" and the US Constitution, we live in a republic. And there is a *big* difference between the two. In reading the Constitution, nowhere does the word "democracy" appear. Yet, how often are we told our country is one? World War I and World War II were fought, "to make the world safe for democracy." The difference between the two systems of government is distinct and clear. A democracy is rule by the majority. Whatever the majority of the voters want, they get. Any group large or small could be a democracy, even a mob. Ever hear of "mob-rule"? Just because the majority votes a certain way, doesn't mean they are right or have the best interests of the people or nation in mind. On the other hand, a republic is a nation of laws that everyone is bound to follow and obey, regardless of their personal opinions. The founding fathers talked and argued long and hard about which type of government should be established. They decided that a republic was the best form of government. A republic was agreed to primarily because *everyone* was to be treated equally under the law with no regard to political connections, size of bank account, or any other potential advantage one might have over another.

One nation under God...

One people, united as a nation, a country. Our rights, which are guaranteed by our Constitution, were originally given to us by God, our creator. The founding fathers believed this and patterned our civil laws after God's laws. These laws and rights are our nation's laws, the source of which is our creator.

Indivisible...

United, not divided. One nation, one people working together for the common good, not individuals or groups fighting to get their way and imposing their way on others. Freedom means the right to choose what is best for you within the boundaries of law and order; the right to believe in something that others may disagree with. The Civil War proved our nation could not be divided, even though there was much division in people's opinions about states' rights and slavery. The Vietnam War also proved we can have our differences of opinion and survive as a nation. September 11, 2001, proved just how united our country *really* is.

With liberty and justice for all.

Freedom and equality, liberty and justice, for everyone. We all have the same chance to do what we want and can. We may not have the same (equal) skills and abilities, but we have an equal opportunity to develop the skills we do have. We may not have the same (equal) ambition or priorities, which means some of us will work to achieve greatness, or wealth, or position, while others may be satisfied just to make ends meet. Yet we all have the same protections under our judicial system. That was the way our nation was founded. That was and is the intent of our founding fathers. It is up to us to maintain it.

—hd

Why is it important we have a pledge to our flag? It is easy to say the words and not understand what we are saying.

Life's Turning Point

There's a turning point in every life,
away from trouble, gloom, and strife.
The road to take is smooth and fair.
The funny thing is, it has always been there.
The signs are clear, if we only look,
all mapped out in one Great Book.

But traffic blinds us, and we lose our way.
We're much to frantic to stop and pray,
so we keep going, alone and afraid,
running farther away from the mess we've made
of this beautiful life, so sweet and brief.

But we do we do? We fill it with grief,
the unfulfilled dream,
the love turned aside,
the hurt and the anger,
the wounded pride.

Oh Lord, make us stop, and make us
see the way you planned it
and meant it to be.

Source: Bonnie J. O'Brien

The reality of life strikes everyone sooner or later. As children and youth, we are concerned with growing up and receiving an education, so we can make our mark in the world. As young adults, our youthful innocence and idealism steadies and guides us to achieve our goals. We get caught up in the road to success. But we weren't prepared for the bumps, sharp turns, and chuckholes found in the road of life. Maybe our goals were set too high or our idealism was unrealistic. Then like the fork in the road, we see the smooth, beautiful, clear road, but we're in the wrong lane, and we can't get over to it. The gloom and strife of reality blinds us. Try as we might, we can't stop. Or can we? We want that smooth, beautiful, clear road, but we're caught in the increasingly hectic mess of materialism, our egos, and our pride.

As we continue to travel our chosen road of life, we see the other road clearly. Looking back, we notice it's always been there, close, but just out of reach. We recall the numerous times we could have changed our direction, wanted to, but just didn't. Is it too late now? Has there been too much hurt caused by us? Too much anger? Too much pride? Do we even know how much of these we've caused? Dare we think we still have a chance? What will others think? Does it really matter?

Life's turning point, we all reach it, some sooner, some later. It's up to us, each one of us, to make the right move. To follow the map made for us in the one Great Book.

—hd

Think of reasons we need to experience hardships and difficult times. Why are these important to our faith journey?

The Lesson of the Eagle and the Fish

Jesus said, "Come, follow me, and I will make you fishers of men."

Matthew 4:19

The fish was swimming through the clear, cool water searching for food, wary of any predator, which might also be searching for food, in particular him. Hours passed, and the fish, ever watchful, fulfilled his needs for nourishment. Several times he successfully avoided his natural enemies. Content, happy, and satisfied, he was suddenly grabbed. From out of nowhere, an eagle found him and pulled the fish out of the water. Twisting and turning, trying to free himself, he saw the widespread wings of the eagle that carried him higher and higher. The eagle, sighting land near his nest, swooped low over the water and landed on a branch, pinning the frantic fish between the rough bark and his powerful claws. The fish looked up at his captor and said in soft but strong voice, "Do you know what I am?"

The eagle, somewhat startled, looked at his catch. "Yeah, dinner."

"No, well, maybe," the fish said, still struggling to break free. "But do you know what I really am?"

"A fish, one of an eagle's favorite meals."

"Hey! You're not listening or thinking."

"Look, fish, I am an eagle. I fly all over looking for food. Today you're dinner, a lowly fish to feed the mighty eagle."

"I may be humble, but I'm not lowly. A humble fish was chosen long ago as the symbol for—"

"A symbol? The lowly fish? *No!* I am a symbol. I fly and soar and rule the skies all over the earth. I alone control my life. It is I who was chosen as the symbol of strength, power, fortitude, and might; I who must be strong to fly far and wide through storms to find food. It is I who lives in the tree tops, braving fierce winds. It is I who was chosen to symbolize the strength of the mighty Roman Empire. It is I who was chosen by governments and empires through out history, including the Untied States of America. Strength, power, fortitude, and might, that is what I symbolize. And you? Just *what* do you symbolize, oh *lowly* and *humble* fish?"

"Many things, goodness, mercy, love."

"You're still dinner to an eagle."

"Maybe so, but listen. A long time ago there was a man who taught what life was all about. His followers, who were dedicated to Him and His teachings, were often persecuted, beaten, and even killed. To avoid their enemies, they would draw a fish in the sand or dirt to identify themselves. Slowly over the years, decades, and centuries, these followers grew in number. The empire that persecuted and killed many of this teacher's early followers collapsed and crumbled. Upon the ruins of the once mighty Roman Empire grew one of the centers of the followers of this great teacher. I may be dinner to you, but what I symbolize has lasted longer than any government or empire you symbolize. You said you are the symbol of strength, power, fortitude, and might. Listen to this, then do what you must, 'But they that wait upon the Lord shall renew their strength, they shall mount up with wings as eagles, they shall run and not be weary, they shall walk and not faint,' (Isaiah 40:31)."

The eagle listened carefully then flew to his nearby nest, giving the fish to his growing brood.

While sitting and watching, this mighty eagle thought about what the fish had said. That lowly fish was right! Empires collapsed that used the eagle as their symbol. Yet, the symbolic fish and what it stood for (and still stands for) did indeed flourish. Not only flourish, but it gave *substance* and *nourishment* to the mighty and powerful.

The lesson?

No matter how strong, how powerful and mighty, no matter how free and independent or in control we are or may become, our *substance* and *nourishment* comes from the humble fish, which symbolizes our belief and our faith in Jesus Christ, who said, "Come, follow me..."

Source: Herbert Dettmer.

This is a story for a discussion of pride, personal status, humility, natural order, and has religious symbolism. Try to think about the symbolism more deeply.

Psalm 100

Make a joyful noise unto Jehovah, all ye lands.

Serve Jehovah with gladness:

Come into His presence with singing.

Know ye that Jehovah, He is God:

It is He that hath made us, and we are His;

We are His people and the sheep of His pasture.

Enter into His gates with thanksgiving,

and into His courts with praise.

Give thanks unto Him and bless His name.

For Jehovah is good; His loving kindness endureth forever.

And His faithfulness unto all generations.

Source: Herbert Fish's personal Bible

"Make a joyful noise..." *Right!* Just what we need in this world is more noise, of any kind—joyful or otherwise. Cars, trucks, motorcycles, stereos, lawnmowers, airplanes, people talking loudly next door, and any other kind of sound we might consider noise. What we need is *less* noise, not more. How often have any of us commented while enjoying a walk in the park, "How nice is it here; how quiet"?

In the office, the factory, the warehouse, or wherever we work, the phones, the fax, the copiers, the computer printers all contribute to our elevated stress levels. At home the phone rings, our neighbor is working in his yard cutting the grass or trimming the bushes, all of which contribute more to the noise-annoyance factor. Yet, the psalmist says, we should make more. "Make a joyful noise…"

A joyful noise? Joy and noise don't seem to be compatible. Maybe the psalmist knows something we don't. (Maybe?) But the psalmist lived way back when, before modern society, before power equipment for everything; before snow blowers, lawnmowers, race cars, trains, and airplanes; before amplifiers and electronic gizmos for work and play. Would the psalmist write the same words today?

"Make a joyful noise unto the Lord." Praise God, for without Him where would we be? We wouldn't be here or anywhere without God. He created us, gave us life, and gave us our home on earth. We are His and His alone. As He loves us, we should love Him. Doesn't the Bible say, "Love the Lord your God?"

"Make a joyful noise unto the Lord." Love God. Be thankful for what we have. Modern language and our understanding of what words mean have been changing throughout history. The keyword here is *joyful*. Subtle and not so subtle changes in our language have distorted the original and real meaning of words written long ago. But on reflection the word we see and hear still should guide us, teach us, and maybe even inspire us.

Still the psalmist says, "joyful noise." Joyful—happy and pleasing; noise—sound of some kind, singing perhaps? The Lord our God wants us to be active in our service and worship. Maybe our noise could be repairing the house (or car) of someone in need of our help. Whatever our "noise" might be, in praising our Lord from our hearts because we truly believe what we are saying and doing.

"Make a *joyful* noise…"

—hd

Are there any "noises" that can be comforting?

Be

Be understanding to your enemies
and loyal to your friends.

Be strong enough to face the world each day
and weak enough to know you cannot do everything alone.

Be generous to those who need your help
and frugal with what you need yourself.

Be wise enough to know that you do not know everything and foolish enough to believe in miracles.

Be willing to share your joys
and to share the sorrows of others.

Be a leader when you see the path that others missed and a follower when you are shrouded by the mists of uncertainty.

Be the first to congratulate an opponent who succeeds and the last to criticize a colleague who fails.

Be sure where your next step will fall
so that you will not stumble.

Be sure of your final destination
in case you area going the wrong way.

Be loving to those who love you,
and to those who do not—they may change.
But above all—

Be yourself.

Source: Anonymous

The verse tells us to "be" many things, all of which can be found in the operator's manual of life, the Holy Bible. With so much turmoil and unhappiness in the world, everyone needs as much help as we can find. What better source than the Bible? To be understanding and loyal, to be strong and weak, takes more comprehension than we often have. The key is to know when—when to be strong and when to be weak, when to be generous and when to be frugal. Sometimes wisdom is easy and foolishness is necessary. To share both the joys and sorrows of life gives us the opportunity to share our love. Knowing when to lead and speak up and when to follow and be silent shows a certain measure of maturity and wisdom.

Those who succeed who we opposed in work or play will respect us more when we offer our congratulations. Maybe next time they will be on our side or team or we on theirs. When a friend fails, offering support and encouragement will ease the pain. We never know when it may be our turn to need a friendly shoulder to cry on.

Keeping our eyes open through the pitfalls of life will help us not to stumble. Whatever our final destination might be, be sure of the way—knowing there is only *one* way. And loving everyone as we were taught by the greatest teacher who ever lived will be returned time and time again by those who have always loved us and even by those who never have. For like the opponent we congratulated, those who never have, may love us some day.

And above all, following the instructions in the operator's manual of life, you will, we all will, "Be yourself."

—hd

Is this all about sharing life experiences with those around us? Be they friend or stranger.

Faith and Fear

Faith is the belief that what you *cannot* see will come to pass.

Fear is the belief that what you *can* see will come to pass.

Source: Unknown

It is easy to believe whatever you can see. A warm spring rain that cleans the air and waters the grass and garden. Or a severe thunderstorm with its damaging winds and lighting. Either is easy to believe. We see it, we experience it, and we maybe even feel it. It's there, reality, right in front of our eyes.

Reality: the fear of what is happening or what could happen. If we drive too fast on a wet or snow- and ice-covered road, we could cause a serious accident. If we touch a burning match or sharp knife, we fear the pain of the burn or cut. Painting the ceiling in our homes or washing the windows on a ladder, we may fall if we're not careful. Yes, we see the slippery road, the hot match, the sharp knife, and the ladder, and we understand the dangers.

But faith is different; we cannot see the seed germinate and start to grow. Yet we know it will soon be a flower or blade of grass. Faith tells us this. We cannot see the healing that takes place in our bodies when we or a loved one is ill or injured. All we can see is the result. Yet we believe in the power of prayer and God's healing hand. This is faith. As the hand of God heals us, all we can see is the result: recovery or death. And isn't death a form of healing? One who has been suffering from some condition or illness is freed of the pain when life leaves the earthly body. That is being healed.

After Jesus arose from the tomb on that first Easter, He appeared to His disciples and showed them His hands. Thomas was not with them, and when told Jesus had risen from the tomb, he said he would only believe when he saw where the nails had pierced His hands. Later, Jesus appeared to Thomas. He put his finger on Jesus' hand and his hand on Jesus' side, only then did Thomas believe. Jesus, the risen Savior, then told him, "Because you have seen me, you believed; blessed are those who have not seen and yet believe" (John 20:19-29). Thomas saw and believed, but not because of faith. Yet many others who had not seen did believe. They had the faith of believing what they could (did) not see.

Faith—believing what we cannot see. "Take it on Faith." Believe in the unexplained, the unseen.

Faith—we cannot see God, and we believe in Him.

Fear—we can see the damaging storm or the sharp blade, and we believe in the danger or potential danger.

Fear is easy, sometimes instinctive, but faith is more powerful and longer lasting.

By being faithful, we need not fear reality.

—hd

What you can't or don't see can and will affect us in ways we may not fully understand.

With Love

I am so very small
and my fingerprints so large
That you sometimes get discouraged
when I leave them on the walls.

But all those messy prints
when I am grown someday
will only be a memory
that will be washed away.

So here's a set of prints
to help you to recall
just how those little hands looked
when they were very small.

Source: Unknown

Any parent with a child over the age of one week will attest to the speed at which their children grow. Thinking back, I remember my father's fortieth birthday. As a typical, normal, ten-year-old boy, I looked at him in awe and said with love in my heart, "Forty! That's old!" His reply was a good-natured, fatherly laugh. Thirty years later on an unusually warm, late-March afternoon, I sat on the front porch of my home, my own children scurrying around getting ready for "Daddy's party." My parents arrived, and Mom greeted me with a hug, kiss, and a "Happy Birthday." Then Dad, still twenty feet away, said in loving, fatherly way, "Forty! That's old!"

The handprints I left on the walls when I was ten were much smaller than my hands are today. The hands of my children are much larger now than they were when I held them as newborns. Time marches on, children grow up, parents grow older. The ten-year-old boy of years ago grew up: high school, college, military service, job, career, marriage, and now with children of his own; can't help but remember, he can't help but wonder.

Time marches on; nothing can stop it. Enjoy today. Learn from yesterday's mistakes, and cherish the memories made today. Soon, sooner than any of us will be ready to hear, our grandchildren say to our children with love, "Forty! That's old!"

—hd

Time marches on, quickly, so very quickly. It has been said, "Time flies when you're having fun." As we get older we realize time flies all the time.

A Mother's Meditation (Number 1)

My walls, they may have fingerprints,
my windows may have streaks,
my carpet, it needs a cleaning,
and my kitchen faucet leaks.

My bathroom floor could use some help,
and some tiles could use some glue.
The ironing will get done—someday,
when I have a week or two.

My kitchen floor could tell some tales,
of meals of long ago.
The stove really should be cleaned,
maybe in a month or so.

But let me tell you about my kids.
I haven't mentioned them yet.
At the ripe old age of only three,
they knew their alphabet.
They know the love of our dear Lord,

Herbert Dettmer

and say their prayers each night,
with Mom and Dad kneeling ever so close
to tell them all will be right.

Source: Rebecca Dettmer

Our house wasn't always like the poem described. It was clean, maybe not spotless, but clean. Our children learned and played and were otherwise normal children. Our home was often the base for activities of the friends of our kids, throughout their growing-up years. Parties, barbeques, sleepovers, and the site for pictures for homecoming and proms were often at our house.

Even with the normal trials and problems of teenagers, our house seemed to be the center for many youth and adult activities. Yes, we had an active home. And all the while, our friends as well as our kids' friends always felt comfortable there. Why? Maybe because our house was centered around our heavenly Father and His Son.

Ours wasn't the only home like this. There were many, and are many, where there was a good, positive, and comfortable environment for the family. All had as their center God and Jesus. Could that be the reason our family was not on the local police blotter? Is that the reason many other homes aren't?

—hd

Mothers are very special people with feelings and emotions their children cannot imagine and fathers rarely understand.

'Twas the Night Before (Number 1)

'Twas the night before Jesus came, and all through the house, no one had been praying, not a soul in the house.

Their Bibles were all stuck in the drawer without care, in hopes that Jesus would not come there.

The children were all nestled, all snug in their beds, not once ever kneeling or bowing their heads.

And Mom in her kerchief and I in my cap
had just settled down for a long winter's nap.

When out of the east there rose such a clatter,
I sprang to my feet to see what was the matter.
Away to the door I flew like a flash,
tore open the window and threw up the sash.

When what to my wondering eyes should appear, but angels proclaiming that Jesus was here!

With a light like the sun sending a ray,
I knew in a moment it must be *the* day.

The light of His face made me turn my head.
It was Jesus of Nazareth, alive, risen from the dead.
And though I had mountains of this world's wealth, I cried when I saw Him, in spite of myself.

In the book of life that He held in His hand,
was written in blood the name of every saved man.
He spoke not a word, as He searched for my name.
When He said, "It's not written," my head hung in shame.

The people whose names had been written in blood,
He gathered to take to His Father above.
With those that were saved, He rose without a sound,
while those who rejected Him were left standing 'round.

I fell to my knees just moments too late.
I had waited too long and thus sealed my fate.
I stood and cried as they rose out of sight.
Oh, if only I had been ready tonight.

In reading this poem the meaning is clear:
the returning of Jesus is drawing quite near.

Source: An unknown poet

In our increasingly secular world, where "image" and "appearance" are so vitally important, have we forgotten the source of life itself? Our society has become so advanced in all areas that there is too little time for the appreciation of life. We work hard to earn a living and provide for our physical needs. To keep up with the ever-increasing and expanding technology we must study, perhaps even return to school to learn how to use this new technology. With information networks stretching worldwide, we are told what happens one thousand miles away will affect us. We must be prepared for rising and falling interest rates or how a natural disaster will affect prices at the store—to compete in an ever-changing global community and to forget what we learned last week or even yesterday. Businesses advertise constantly for our hard-earned money. Nonprofit groups solicit donations for their cause. We must spend more and more time and money for education and be ever aware of what we do or say to avoid a lawsuit. But before any of that, we must pay our taxes to every level of government.

The harder we work, the more we learn, the more we do, it's never enough. So we continue running along learning more, earning more, doing more, and paying more. Some can barely keep up, while others are able to advance in careers and accumulate wealth. Yet none of us–or few of us—apparently see and try to understand beyond our immediate needs. Even our churches are often caught up in this never-ending cycle.

Yet we learned about the second coming of Jesus. How and when it will happen, no one knows. What can we do about it? We're too busy maintaining our images, appearances, and lifestyles. We go to church only when it's convenient or "necessary." The Bible is too hard to understand and often boring. There are a hundred reasons, maybe a thousand, why we don't read the Bible. Besides, what was written thousands of years ago doesn't necessarily apply to today's world, or does it? There are many excuses and reasons why we don't pay closer attention to what's *really* important.

Only at times of serious injury or illness or during some personal or national crises or tragedy do we turn to God for comfort and understanding.

"'Twas the night before..." This parody of the well-known Christmas story has a clear message. How many of us will be ready? How many of us are ready now? How many of us will hear the words, "It's not written?"

—hd

Talk about how the "rat race" of life affects the most important part of our existence.

Thoughts on Being a Christian

A true Christian is one who feels
God treats him better than he should be treated.
So he treats others better than they should be
treated.

Source: H. D. Fish

Following the teachings of Jesus and living as true Christians in our modern society is very difficult, to say the least, and sometimes nearly impossible. We see fraud, waste, and hypocrisy everywhere. We see our friends and associates doing things we believe are wrong and getting away with them.

Try as we do to lead a Christian life, temptation often clouds our better judgment. Yet we do remember the golden rule. Try as we might, too often we have fallen short of what we should and should not do. Still, God loves us and always "treats us better" than we should be treated, giving us an example to follow to "treat others better than they should be treated."

—hd

(See The Ten Commandments.)

The Ten Commandments

Thou shalt have no other gods before me. Thou shalt not make unto thee a graven image, nor any likeness of anything that is in heaven above, or that is in the earth beneath, or that is in the water under the earth.

Thou shalt not bow down thyself to them nor serve them. . .

Thou shalt not take the name of Jehovah thy God in vain. . .

Remember the Sabbath day, to keep it holy. . .

Honor thy father and thy mother. . .

Thou shalt not kill. . .

Thou shalt not commit adultery. . .

Thou shalt not steal. . .

Thou shalt not bear false witness against thy neighbor. . .

Thou shalt not covet thy neighbor's house. . .

Source: H. D. Fish's personal Bible

The Ten Commandments where given to Moses by God, as the basic rule and law for the Hebrew people, during the return to the promised land. These laws were not intended to be merely *suggestions* or general guidelines for personal behavior; they were (and are) *Commandments*. God said, "Thou shalt not..." That should be clear enough to anyone who believes or claims to believe.

"Thou shalt have no other gods before me." There is only one god, our God, our Creator, who created the universe and all that is in heaven above, the earth beneath, and in the water under the earth. Everything we can see, hear, or touch was created by God. Even that which we cannot see, hear, or touch, He created. We should keep everything in creation in its proper perspective, with God at the top, in the highest position. For without Him, we wouldn't be.

"Thou shalt not bow down thyself to them, nor serve them." All of God's creations were put here for a specific purpose, for mankind to use for those intended purposes, not to be worshiped or otherwise served. Only God our Creator is to be worshiped and served. In other words, we should worship the Creator, not the creation or anything in it.

"Thou shalt not take the name of Jehovah thy God in vain." As believers in Jehovah—God—we should show the proper and utmost respect and reverence to Him. One way is not to use His name in any manner that would reflect anything but the highest and purest thoughts, words, and deeds for our creator. "Glory to God in the Highest," is often heard at church services.

Using His name in any way, other than in prayer, study, or worship should be absolutely avoided.

"Remember the Sabbath day, to keep it holy." The Sabbath day for most Christians is Sunday, but even if a Christian group chooses Saturday or any other day as the Sabbath, it should be a day of worship and rest and not a day for work. It should be a *special* day set aside for God.

"Honor thy father and thy mother." We were "given" to our parents by God to nurture, teach, and grow. No matter what the circumstances of our birth might be, our parents, whether biological or adoptive or foster, are our parents and should be held in high respect and honor. Without them, we as little children would have little if any chance to survive and grow up to be parents ourselves.

"Thou shalt not kill." *Intentionally* ending the life of a living creature is *not* to be done. But does this mean if we kill a plant or animal for food are we guilty of breaking this commandment? No, since plants and animals were put on earth for the purpose of providing nourishment, shelter, and clothing for us. See the creation story in Genesis, especially Chapter 1:26-30. Any other reason for killing *is* violating this commandment.

"Thou shalt not commit adultery." God created us because He loves us. Love is the most powerful emotion we have. To love another, as in marriage or a committed relationship, to be truly blessed by God, must be completely monogamous. Only one for each of us, just as there was in the garden of Eden—Adam and Eve. To seek pleasure or comfort with another while married destroys the vows made, the commitment to each other, and to God.

"Thou shalt not steal." In the simplest terms possible, if it's not yours, don't touch it. If you don't touch it, you can't take it. And if you don't take it, you're not going to steal it. If one must have something belonging to someone else, ask for permission to borrow it. But taking something that belongs to another without their knowing you are taking it is stealing. This could be something tangible or intangible. Time, for example, is too often "stolen" from one's employer by not working while on the clock or even not working at the pace that is necessary to get the job done.

"Thou shalt not bear false witness." Spreading falsehoods about anyone or anything, telling a lie or exaggerating for your own benefit whether in a positive or negative way is not the way God says we should live or act. Being *completely* honest with everyone and ourselves is not always easy. Honesty can hurt people's feelings, but lying or telling something that is not true can be just as hurtful, maybe even more. If everyone were honest all the time, think how much better our world–God's world–would be, if all of us followed this commandment, all the time.

"Thou shalt not covet." To covet, or to wish for something belonging to another, is wrong. Maybe your neighbor earned what you wanted, or maybe he didn't. It doesn't matter how he obtained it; it's his, not yours. If you want the same thing he has, go out and earn the money so you can buy one of your own. If it is something that cannot be bought, his wife for example, you're just out of luck. There are too many other variables that make this example out of our hands.

The Ten Commandments are God's rules and laws for all believers to live by. All other rules or laws are secondary to these Commandments. But any other rule or law given to us by God supports and enforces the Commandments. We should be diligent in understanding them and living by them. They are *laws,* "must dos," not merely suggestions or guidelines. Most start by saying, "Thou shalt not..." What part of "Thou shalt not..." don't we understand?

—hd

How often do we think about these while going about our everyday tasks? Do we truly try to follow each of these?

The Twenty-Third Psalm

The Lord is my shepherd; I shall not want.

He maketh me to lie down in green pastures;

He leadeth me beside still waters.

He restoreth my soul:

He leadeth me in the paths of righteousness for His name's sake.

Yea, though I walk through the valley of the shadow of death,

I will fear no evil; for Thou art with me.

Thy rod and thy staff, they comfort me.

Thou preparest a table before me, in the presence of mine enemies:

Thou annointest my head with oil;

My cup runneth over.

Surely goodness and mercy shall follow me all the days of my life;

And I will dwell in the house of the Lord forever.

Source: King James Version of the Holy Bible

Throughout each day, as we go about our own routines, often problems arise. Usually minor ones, which can be resolved without much more than a phone call or a few words. Hardly even a thought of our Shepherd is needed for these problems. Yet when a major problem or crisis confronts us, we always run to Him for help, and maybe not "always."

We are constantly striving in our modern society to be self-sufficient and independent. Our jobs, careers, families, and friends take much, perhaps most, of our time and energy. When we do find time for reflection and prayer, how many of us just go through the motions of worship? We can read or recite the Psalm with a clear understanding. Or can we? Do we fully understand what the psalmist is saying?

Our Lord is indeed our shepherd, leader, inspiration, protector, and provider. If we *truly* follow Him, He will care for us and guide us just as a shepherd does with his sheep. The sheep follow their shepherd, just as we follow our Lord. We only need to be observant enough to see the green pastures and still waters set before us. Although even if we look close, sometimes we still can't see them. We only need to stop long enough to restore our souls and listen as He gives us guidance in the paths of goodness. Listen, pay attention, and *understand*. Don't just *hear*. And just what are the green pastures, and where can we find the still waters? In the park? Out in the country, far away from the hectic city life? Or could we find these in the midst of chaos and confusion? Are these green pastures wherever we make the effort to slow down and listen to take a break from the rat race? Still waters to calm our weary minds and bodies, is it symbolism? Or have we missed the point of this familiar Psalm?

The expression, "You can lead a horse to water, but you can't make him drink," may be an appropriate thought. Our shepherd provides us, leads us, to quiet green pastures where still waters would calm and refresh us—restore us. The shepherd is ready, but are we? He is ready to give us rest and refreshment—physical, yes, but spiritual too. We only need to be receptive and like that horse, to drink of the water He provides for us.

How many dangers lurk around us as we blindly walk through the dark shadows? If we accept Him, believe in Him, our shepherd will protect us and comfort us with His rod and staff. Is this more symbolism? A human shepherd protects his flock from the wolves and other predators with a rod and staff. Our Shepherd, our Lord, protects and comforts us, His flock, with what? His rod and staff, which is His Love.

Our enemies may mock us. May? They will! They will challenge us, even dare us as we sit at our shepherd's table. Our enemies cannot comprehend why we sit resting when there is work to be done. Yet our enemies are blind to our shepherd's care and love for us and for them.

Our heads are anointed. Is this more symbolism? Baptism? And our cups overflow (hearts full of love?), and our enemies still mock us. They don't understand what good there is in being good. Though we may stray from the path, our shepherd is there waiting for our return. What good is there in being good? Can we take better care of ourselves? Or do we just think we can? Our shepherd is waiting. When we do return is there some reason, some reward? As the psalmist says, "… and I will dwell in the house of the Lord forever."

—hd

Think about the valley, dark shadows, still waters, green pastures, a rod and a staff in today's world. What are they, and how do they influence our lives?

A Man

He was born in an obscure village.

He worked in a carpenter's shop until he was thirty.

He then became an itinerant preacher;

He never held an office.

He never had a family, or owned a house.

He didn't go to college.

He had no credentials but Himself.

All the armies that ever marched,

All the navies that ever sailed,

All the parliaments that ever sat,

And all the kings that ever reigned,

Have not affected the life of mankind as much as He...

Twenty centuries have come and gone and today

He is still the central figure of the human race...

Jesus Christ

Source: Unknown

We are constantly reminded of the need to be secure and successful. Job and career performance, prudent investment of time and money, and continuing education we are told will assure success and financial security. Numerous opportunities abound to enable us to "make it to the top." With all the schemes, plans, and methods available to achieve whatever we want or desire, the only factor missing is our own efforts to "plan the work and work the plan." It takes individual effort before anything will happen. Networking with friends and associates benefits all who participate. Yet too often all the effort, time, money, and desire fail to produce the results we are searching for. So we rework and reorganize or maybe just start over. Some people equate not reaching goals either short-term or long-term with failure. Many quit striving, while others just quit, discouraged and disgusted. With all the planning and working to be successful, with all the schemes, plans, and methods available, how many people have studied the most successful man who ever lived?

This man born to "working-class" parents who at the time of his birth were homeless and not married. Yet despite this, he was destined for, shall we say, greatness? After all, didn't the brightest star shine over His humble birthplace? He learned a trade and worked at it for years before becoming what today might be considered a faith healer, a street-corner preacher or perhaps a radical revisionist. With no money or income to support himself, with no spouse or family, he had nothing. Nothing except for who He was.

From that humble beginning, He gathered twelve men and traveled throughout the country. With these twelve men—His network—people came to listen, to be healed, and to be saved. Starting with those men, an empire was built, which has withstood wars, famine, persecution, traitors, dictators, both natural and man-made disasters, and even the test of time. His followers then and now have believed, suffered, and even died for Him.

Today, twenty centuries after His death on the cross (in today's words He was executed), there are more of His followers—Christians—in the world than followers or believers of any other faith.

Was Jesus Christ successful? *Is* He successful? The answer lies within each of us.

—hd

Dare we try to compare anyone in history who has influenced life as we know it as much as Jesus Christ?

What I Asked For

I asked God for strength, that I might achieve—
I was made weak, that I might learn to obey.

I asked for health, that I might do greater things—

I was given infirmity, that I might do better things.

I asked for riches, that I might be happy—
I was given poverty, that I might be wise.

I asked for power, that I might have the praise of men—

I was given weakness, that I might feel the need of God.

I asked for all these things, that I might enjoy life—

I got nothing I asked for—but everything I hoped for.

Almost despite myself, my unspoken prayers were answered.

I am, among all men, most richly blessed.

Source: An unknown disabled veteran

Our goal-oriented, success-driven society has enabled many to achieve and acquire much more than previous generations. We have bigger, nicer homes and better cars and more time for recreational activities and community service. With our computers and other hi-tech marvels, there isn't anything we as individuals or a society can do. Increased awareness of nutrition and health has made us stronger and healthier. Opportunities abound for the acquisition of money, financial security, and material possessions. With those comes the admiration of others, perhaps even envy. With all we have, we somehow think we need more, deserve more. So we continue to strive for more of what we already have. Never satisfied, onward and upward we go, setting new and higher goals for ever greater rewards. Then, still working and striving onward, we look back (or perhaps down?) and wonder how some other people can live on so much less.

Could it be "they" understand life better? Could "they" know something we don't? Could "they" have an understanding of life we don't even know exists? Maybe the author of this verse, a disabled military veteran, learned something while he was fighting for our freedom? Or while recovering from his wounds?

We look at the "strength" of our assets—our education, our career position—knowing the hard work it took to get where we are. And we just don't understand why some people, though they appear weak, are content and happy with life.

Our healthy lifestyles with nutritious food and exercise enable us to do so much. Yet there are others who seem to be making a real difference.

Happiness assured by all our possessions seems to pale when we see some people with so much less appearing to be much more satisfied with life. Do they know something we don't?

The positions of authority—of power—we have, make our peers congratulate us, and we look upon others with dismay or even pity. Sometimes we'll say they are lazy or perhaps lack the needed skills, education, and ambition to better themselves. We mistake their bowed heads for weakness. We don't recognize their humility.

How different our lives are, ours and theirs. All the comforts, security, and toys we enjoy, yet they seem to have more than we do. Not that we'd ever admit, "they" are more richly blessed.

—hd

We ask for many things, not just material items, and often receive something different. But somehow our *needs* are satisfied.

Lonely Hours

Sometimes, in the lonely hours,
when I come to grips with life,
I think of all I've left undone,
as a daughter, sister, mother, and wife.

If I could have a second chance,
how different it would be.
How each day I would enhance,
the joys that came to me.

The sun of life is setting now.
As each day closes,
how fervently I wish
I had taken time to smell the roses.

Source: Edith Podreskey

We never get a second chance to make a first impression, that all-important first impression at a job interview, the first date with our future spouse, or the first meeting with a new client; that critical first impression. Though often we find ourselves in less than a desirable position, we can't change how others see us that first time. Never are we given a second chance to make a better first impression.

Reflecting on one's day or week is much the same. We never get a second chance to live *today* over or this week. Of all the things we've done, could we have done them better? Faster? Slower? Could we have done something we didn't but should have? Of all the things we did, was there something we shouldn't have done? Acts of commission and omission can be equally hurtful. A forgotten friend or relative in need of company or just a word of encouragement; lonely hours when no one seems to care. The older man or woman living alone, their spouse having passed on; the traveler between flights in a crowded airport; the soldier or marine far from home; the child at summer camp for the first time, that first night when all is quiet. Lonely hours, when for some reason we can't sleep, with children in bed across the hall, and spouse close by, all sleeping peacefully while we lie awake. Was there something left undone? Unsaid? Was there something we didn't do as well as we could have? Should have?

What joy we could bring if only we had a second chance to live today over. What hurt could we avoid if only? What effort would it take? How much time? What good would it do for them or for us?

The first impression, a second chance, today is over. Could we have done better? Or more? Or less?

The Rose Lady reflects on her long and full life. Her mother long ago had passed on; her sister not long ago had passed on, her husband too. Lonely hours sitting, thinking, remembering the good times with daughter, granddaughter, then great-grandchildren. Yes, the good times.

Lonely hours, a time to reflect on our lives; lonely hours at the end of the day or near the end of our lives. Could we have done more? Could we have made a better first impression?

Could we have taken the time to smell the roses?

—hd

In our busy lives, crowded with people we know and don't know, how and why are so many people lonely?

The Contagious Smile

Smile awhile—
While you smile—
another smiles;
and soon there are miles
and miles of smiles.
And life's worth while
if you but smile.

Source: A World War II era song,
H. D. Fish collection

Smiles, those friendly expressions everyone likes to see and share when greeting friends, family, and even strangers. Maybe especially strangers, for they may become friends one day.

A smile expresses a special warmth that cannot be mistaken. In times of anger, people rarely smile. During any argument or confrontation, verbal or otherwise, smiles are rarely seen. How much joy and happiness is there during any confrontation? How many might have been avoided if someone would just *smile?*

One smile is all it would take to start, then another, and another. Soon the anger eases. Perhaps people would talk instead of argue. It's hard—no, impossible—

to be angry when there is joy and happiness all around us. Smiling gives us what we need to calm the anger.

Though sadness, disappointment, and grief are unavoidable during our lives, the smile of a friend or loved one helps to ease our pain. While we grieve a loss, a smile tells us someone cares. There is no time when a smile *causes* any negative feeling. A smile is not always appropriate at a funeral or the site of a tragedy, but a smile from someone will always help heal and help soothe the hurt. While tears are a release of a painful loss, a smile does feel better.

With all the hatred and pain in our world today, a smile passed from one to another, to another, could help to stop the spread of negative emotions. If we would smile more often, soon there could be, would be, "miles and miles of smiles."

Smiles for family, friends, and, yes, even strangers, especially strangers. Smiles full of caring, compassion, and love. Love, like a smile, never started an argument, or a war, and never caused pain. A smile like love spreads joy and happiness.

Today, as much as during World War II when this song was written, there is much pain and suffering. Pain, suffering, and hate that can be eased by smiles, "miles and miles of smiles."

—hd

A smile is a universal expression. No matter what language we speak, or what culture we live in, a smile is known by all mankind as a pleasant and happy expression. What other positive expressions are there that communicate happiness?

A Mother's Meditation (Number 2)

A young man stands before the judge alone and afraid. A young girl huddles on a deserted bench in a bus depot. Somewhere a young man lies near death following an overdose of drugs. Somewhere a young girl, left alone by her boyfriend, contemplates which would be better: an abortion or suicide.

Where are the parents of these young people? More importantly, where were they when these young people were growing up? Were the parents too concerned about careers and material things to notice their children? To care and love and guide them. Were they too busy to realize, maybe there was a problem? Did Mom set aside time to make brownies for the Girl Scout troop? Did Dad pass on a golf outing to watch a little league game? God asks us to be fruitful and multiply. But a flower not properly cared for withers and sooner or later dies. Our children are our flowers—our precious blooms grow from just a tiny seed. These flowers must be guarded and treated lovingly in order to grow and mature. We must be there to kiss the bruises, make the mud pies, suffer the name calling, praise the accomplishments, and discipline the misbehavior.

If we as parents don't pay attention to our children when they are young, we won't have them when—and if—they grow to adulthood.

Source: Rebecca Dettmer.

"Mom" is thinking again. Worrying about her children, in ways dads can't imagine.

Kindness and Praise

Forget each kindness that you do,
as soon as you've done it.
Forget the praise that falls on you,
the moment you've won it.
Forget the slander that you hear,
before you can repeat it.
Forget each slight, each spite, each sneer,
whenever you may meet it.

Remember every kindness done to you,
whatever its measure.
Remember praises by others won,
and pass them on with pleasure.
Remember every promise made,
and keep it to the letter.
Remember those who lend you aid,
and be a grateful debtor.

Remember all the happiness,
that comes your way in living.
Forget each worry and distress,
be hopeful and forgiving.

Remember good, remember truth,
remember Heaven's above you.
And you will find, through youth and age,
that many hearts will love you.

Source: H. D. Fish

My, aren't we something! We helped someone in need then quickly patted ourselves on the back. We told our friends and associates what we did, listening to their praise of our marvelous deeds. When we heard that rumor about some scandalous behavior, how quickly we told all who would listen. That's the *reality* of the *real* world.

Is it now? How quickly we've forgotten the difference between the secular world we live in and the world God intended for us. How others see us, how important is it really? And how important is it compared to how God sees us?

Are we so *insecure* we need to talk—brag—about our good deeds? Wouldn't it be better if we could do something positive—a kind word, a helping hand, a donation—and not *expect* accolades (or a tax deduction)? What about the negatives we hear or see? Do we *have* to repeat them? What good does it do? Maybe we feel better about ourselves by repeating them. Or maybe we feel less guilty about our own shortcomings and mistakes. Everyone has good days and bad days. On our bad days, all of us tend to be spiteful and short with those we meet. Not always are we the reason for other's ill temper, though we may be on the receiving end of it. Give the other guy a break. The favor just may be returned when we need it most. Forgetting the positives we do and the negatives we hear and see will have rewards—maybe not immediately and maybe not in the way we might want, but the rewards will be there. "What goes around comes around."

Remembering what good is done to or for us, regardless of how small, remembering the deeds of others, keeps us thinking good thoughts. Follow through with each promise we make and in remembering those who have helped us. Everyone feels better hearing good news. A small deed of kindness, a word of encouragement, a favor never hurts. People may not thank you for them, but they won't forget. And they will love you. The difference between good and bad, positive and negative, is greater than the obvious. Our lifestyles and attitudes may or may not be noticed or appreciated by those around us. But the One who knows when a sparrow falls, the One we can't hide from, will always see and hear everything we do.

Before our day comes to meet Him, we must live here on earth. Wouldn't all of us feel better if everyone followed the advice given in this verse?

Remember the good, forget the bad. Remember happiness, forget the distress. God loves each and every one of us. Wouldn't our lives be better—richer—through youth and age if many hearts loved us too?

—hd

A little humility can go a long way. Do we really *need* a "thank you" for our good deeds? Or is the deed itself thanks enough?

Life Is Like a Rose Bush

A rose bush? Yes, look carefully at the average garden rose plant. The stem from the ground to the flower is life. As we grow from childhood through adolescence to adulthood, we are *climbing* that rose stem. Leaves growing out from the stem enable us to reach and pull ourselves up to the next higher level. As we grow through life, we have many opportunities to reach and pull ourselves to new learning experiences, to serve others, and to make choices. Parents and other family members, teachers, clergy, and friends are all there to help us learn if we reach out to them.

But also on this stem are thorns, which hurt when we touch them; sometimes they hurt a lot. Life is full of thorns or hurt, illness, injury, heartache, disappointment, and loss of a loved one. All of these hurt but are all part of life. And these too can be learning experiences.

As we approach the top of the stem, it bends from our weight; it isn't as strong as it was further down, closer to the base. But then, neither are we. We're getting older; our health may be failing. It takes us longer to heal from illness or injury.

Then one day, we see the rose at the top; this beautiful flower, fragrant, and strong. "What is this?" we ask. Suddenly we realize that only an understanding, loving God could create such beauty. And like when we were a child being held in our mother's arms, we are now in God's arms forever.

Source: Herbert Dettmer.

The continuity of life culminates in heaven. Life is not fair and hurts can be the result. Each hurt, though, can be a learning experience.

List examples of learning in the Rose Bush.
List examples of thorns in the Rose Bush.

The Golden Rule

"Do unto others as you would have them do unto you."

Source: Commonly used wording of the world's major religions, for the universality of proper and acceptable individual conduct.

"The Golden Rule," as stated, is universal in its meaning, intent, and spirit throughout the world's major religions. This is a unique thread that unites everyone of all faiths and backgrounds, regardless of other differences we have. Personal behavior—how we live our lives, how we interact with others, and how we act or react to events over which we have little or no control—is foremost in religious belief. The major differences between religions are the rituals of expressing our beliefs.

Hinduism traces its beginnings to before 1000 Bc, in India. The sacred writings include the Vedas, Brahmanas, Bhagavad-Gita, and the Hitopadesa. The Hindu version reads: "Good people proceed while considering that what is best for others is best for themselves."

The Torah is the sacred writing of Judaism. The five books of Moses are the basis for Jewish thought, law, doctrine, and tradition. From the book of Leviticus: "And thou shalt love thy neighbor as thyself."

Buddhism was founded by Siddhartha Gautama, the Buddha. He was originally from India and traveled throughout Southern Asia. Its holy writings are the Tripitakas, the Dhammapada, and the Udanavarga. "Hurt not others with which pains yourself."

Confucianism was founded by the Chinese philosopher Confucius. The Analects, or the Analects of Confucius, are the sacred writings: "That you do not want done to yourself, do not do to others."

Islamism is the religion followed by Moslems, often called Muslims. Islam was founded by Mohammed bin Abdullah about 622 AD. The sacred writing is the Koran: "No one of you is a believer until he loves for his brother what he loves himself."

Christianity is based on the teachings of Jesus Christ, who was born and lived as a Jewish man. The Savior to Christians, Jesus is considered a prophet by numerous non-believers. The sacred writing is the Holy Bible that is divided into two testaments, the Old and the New. The Old Testament is the foundation of Jewish and Christian belief, and the New Testament is the story of Jesus Christ and His disciples. "Therefore all things whatsoever ye would that men should do to you, do ye even so to them."

Throughout the world, across the continents and cultures, millions upon millions of people believe in various religions. Is it possible *all* these people, these believers, are wrong? I think not! Are all of these believers following the universal teachings of "The

Rule"? Are the political leaders of the various nations represented by these religions *practicing* their respective beliefs? Look around the world. To say it is a mess is an understatement. The followers of the world's religions should look at themselves and their leaders and let everyone know they believe *and* practice the golden rule.

As different as these religions are, culturally and spiritually, their underlying beliefs and practices are very similar. One would hope that each believer in each religion practices what is written in the various holy and sacred writings. Each religion listed shares a belief in a single deity. Each has its own unique way of worshipping. Yet, with the golden rule, each shares the belief that only good thoughts, words and deeds are the right way to live.

Maybe the current direction our world is heading would change if *all* followed the golden rule. What do we have to lose? The world situation can only get better, and if it doesn't, have we lost anything? It's better to try and fail than do nothing and succeed. But what if it does work?

It is in the holy writings of all the world's major religions. Who knows? It just might work.

—hd

The universality of the Golden Rule—discussions of this could last forever, and probably should.

Characteristics of One Who Is Growing

He listens to the man who knows.
He never laughs at a new idea.
He cross-examines his dreams.
When others razz him, he laughs.
He avoids bitterness.
He realizes that the man he is to be—
he is becoming every minute.
He lives a forward- and outward-looking life.
He worships God.
He serves humanity.

Source: H. D. Fish

We never stop growing. From the moment of birth—from the moment of conception we are growing and maturing physically, mentally, emotionally, and spiritually. As a child and an adolescent we just can't wait to be a grown-up. We attend school and interact with our peers, our families, and other adults, trying to learn how to be a grownup. We imitate adults and emulate those we think are good role models. We finally graduate from high school and then maybe college, and *bam!* We're adults.

The real world awaits us, and we're ready, at least we think we are. But soon the *reality* of the *real* adult world hits us, and no matter how well prepared we are or think we are…*bam!* We realize, hopefully not too late, there is still more to learn, and not all of it can come from a book or a classroom.

Following this verse carefully will help keep us on track. We know what to do and for the most part how to do it. Our childhood and education behind us, we will continue to grow and learn.

From that first gray hair and that first wrinkle we realize, though we may not admit it, we are still growing older physically, mentally, and emotionally. As smart as we think we are with our education, experience, and computers, we must remember there is always someone, somewhere who knows more. To listen and learn is a lifelong task. To understand better is growing. People laughed at Henry Ford, the Wright brothers, Thomas Edison, and so many of the early pioneers of "modern" technology—technology today we take for granted, but at the time, was as new as the latest innovation we quickly embrace today. The ideas that everyone could afford a car and that people could fly across the country or the ocean were laughed at. Today, these are not even questioned. Fly to the moon and land on it? It was pure science fiction in Henry Ford's day. But today? We've gone beyond that. Laugh at new ideas? People laughed at the transcontinental railroad, the telephone, and space flights. Dare we laugh at what we cannot understand or imagine? Without new ideas our society would become stagnant. New ideas mixed with old traditions are what keep society healthy and growing.

Our youthful dreams and goals may have seemed desirable and attainable when we set them. But now as we've grown and matured, our youthful idealism becomes more realistic. Our dreams and goals may need to be adjusted or changed. Youthful ambition and adult maturity don't always give us the same perspective. Goals and dreams become more realistic in the real world as we learn our limits, as we change our attitudes, as we *grow*. When kidded and teased or razzed about anything, how many react defensively or in anger? What good does it do? Instead laugh. Laugh with those who tease us. It may not be easy, and it may not stop the teasing, but it certainly will avoid any bitterness that can lead to further problems.

Every moment of our lives, every small and large incident we experience, contributes to what we are becoming. No matter what age we may be. A positive outlook and positive attitude will result in a more pleasant, happier life for each of us and for those around us.

Whether we are growing up or growing older, whether life has been kind to us or not, we all continue to grow. Each of us must determine in what direction we grow and make the best of what life gives us. The only constant factor in life is God's love. The public and private worship of God and our service to others will assure us a more pleasant existence as we continue to grow.

—hd

We spend our childhood looking forward to the day we are a "grown-up." When do we realize we are *always* growing? Maturity, emotional and mental, doesn't always follow physical growth.

The Man in the Glass

When you get what you want in your struggle
for self, and the world makes you king for a day.
Just go to the mirror and look at yourself,
and see what that man has to say.

For it isn't your parents, your children, your
wife, whose judgment you must pass.
The fellow whose verdict counts the most in
your life, is the one staring back from the glass.

Some people may think you're a straight-shoot-
ing chum, and call you a wonderful guy.
But the man in the glass says you're only a bum,
if you can't look him straight in the eye.

He's the fellow to please, never mind all the rest,
for he's with you clear up to the end.
And you've passed your most dangerous, dif-
ficult test, if the man in the glass is your friend.

You may fool the whole world down the path-
way of life, and get pats on the back as you pass.

But your final reward will be heartache and tears,
if you've cheated the man in the glass.

Source: An unknown poet

Throughout our lives, we work hard to achieve the numerous goals we have set—long-term, mid-term, and short-term goals. Often these goals must be altered or changed as various circumstances arise. Ideas we had as young men and women may become unrealistic as life teaches us. The real world is much different from the world we knew as adolescents while in school.

As we become spouses and parents, our needs change that can and will change our interests and priorities. Career and job responsibilities increase, more demands are placed on our limited time, and we may seek short-cuts to do everything we need or want to accomplish. Temptation raises its ugly head to "help us."

Money, position, a big home, nice cars, all the modern toys of being successful in today's society are meaningless if we can't look at ourselves in the mirror without saying, "But I had to do that, I wouldn't have been promoted if I didn't." The man (or woman) looking back at us from the mirror knows we should truly follow the principles, standards, and moral behavior we know is the right way to live. The old adage "the end justifies the means" isn't always true, especially if the "means" aren't in keeping with honest principles, standards, and morals.

Parents, children, spouses, friends, associates, and acquaintances all might be impressed with our success, but none of them know us the same way we know us. None of them knows the little lies and shortcuts we may have used to gain an advantage to win, to succeed, not like that face in the mirror looking back at us. We can fool everyone we know (even Mom) and those we don't know, but we can't fool ourselves.

Even blatant justification of our actions and inactions can't change the fact we know we could have done better, perhaps more honestly (*probably* more honestly). No matter what others think of us or our success, no matter if it is good or ill, no one knows what really happened, no one but that face looking back at us from the mirror.

That face can smile and be your friend, or if it's been cheated, the final reward could be more than disappointing. Next time you comb your hair or brush your teeth, take a good, close look at the face looking back at you.

Is that face your friend? If you're not sure, maybe it is not, and only you can do something about it.

—hd

Can we be and are we truly honest with ourselves?

A Thanksgiving Poem

As we lay the bounty of harvest on the altar,
on this Thanksgiving Day,
grateful for the Lord's unending love,
in each and every way,

Let us remember our lives are like the fertile
fields, where each day we sow some seed,
in every thought and action,
in every word and deed.

Let us sow seeds of kindness because,
as we all know,
we can only reap the harvest,
from the seeds we sow.

Source: Edith Podreskey
Printed in the Worship Bulletin,
November 12, 1989
First United Methodist Church
Valparaiso, Indiana
Used with permission

A Thanksgiving Prayer

Lord, for Thy gifts—this more than daily bread—
Wherewith our needs are fed;
for all these bounties, deep and dear and living,
we give our thanksgiving.
As even so, delivered both from famine and foe,
our fathers did three hundred years ago.

Bless us, oh Lord; this house, these children, and
this laden board;
But bless besides, a shelter in Thy hand!
This land, this far reaching land,
that all these are fruits of.

Lord, we pray, wake in our hearts today,
not gratitude alone, but stubborn will.
To guard our dream to watch rampart still
against more difficult odds and darker perils, yes,
and false gods, than pilgrim minds could measure.
Let us then become a lamp to light the world again,
as once we were.

We thank Thee, Lord. Amen

Source: H. D. Fish, November, 1943

Thanksgiving—a turkey dinner with all the trimmings and a football game. Thanksgiving—a trip to Grandma's house for the traditional family get-together. Visit with people we haven't seen since...since when? Last Thanksgiving?

Just what is Thanksgiving? Is it a day to feast on turkey, to visit with relatives and friends, to watch football and a parade? Or is it a day to pause, to reflect, and to give thanks to God for our many, many blessings? God has blessed us in many ways, perhaps in ways we don't even realize. We readily accept these blessings, yet how often do we pause and give thanks to Him? Once a year on the fourth Thursday of November?

Let us digress for a moment. Every basic science book says, "For every action there is an equal and opposite reaction." Every equation in algebra must be kept equal. Change one side, and the same must be done to the other. In every business transaction, there must be a buyer and a seller. For every blessing, there must be a thankful heart. God loves us and gives each of us a bounty of harvest. Do we too often just assume we will continue to receive?

"Every action has an equal and opposite reaction." For every deed done, whether good or bad, there is a reaction. Smiling at a stranger passing us on the street might just make the difference in his life or hers. Maybe that stranger is having a personal crisis or just a bad day. A smile may ease the pain if only for a moment. A kind word to a friend will warm the heart.

Plant a seed of corn and watch the cornstalk grow. Plant a garden, tend it carefully, lovingly, and gather the fruits of your labor for dinner and lunch. Plant a seed of kindness—a thought, word, or deed—and watch the reaction. Plant a seed of spite or hate or evil, and watch the reaction. Which is better? Which will produce a prayer of thanks from that stranger having a crisis or bad day?

For every deed done, there is a reaction. For every item we buy, there must be a seller. For every smile we give a stranger, for every kind word, for every thoughtful deed, a seed is planted, and that seed will grow.

For the bounty of our harvest, no matter if it is the food on our table or our thoughts, words, and deeds, all started sometime, someplace with the planting of a seed. To harvest good, we must plant good seeds, or we can plant seeds of the other kind, for "…we can only reap the harvest from the seeds we sow."

Thanksgiving—a special day to give thanks for the harvest of the good seeds we've planted throughout the year.

—hd

The poem and prayer offer feelings of gratitude for our many blessings. Can we make a list of the "smaller" blessings?

The Gift

One Christmas morning a wife opened a present, a rather large one, although it was very light. It was gaily wrapped and ribboned. Inside was just an empty box, but for a small piece of paper, folded in half. She unfolded the paper and read it:

"This is a symbolic gift.

The box is empty,

as my life would be

without you and your love.

I love you."

Source: Herbert Dettmer

Empty lives, like empty boxes, need to be filled. What to fill either with is the question. A Christmas present wrapped in brilliantly colored paper with a pretty ribbon around it looks nice, maybe even exciting, under the tree. What could be inside? A new warm fuzzy robe? How long will it last? Pretty earrings and matching necklace? How much did these cost? Does it really matter? Isn't it the thought that counts? Thought? What ever happened to love? (Or is it the bigger and more costly the gift is, the more love one shows?)

Empty lives are often full of warm, fuzzy robes, dazzling jewelry, new and even not so new "things." Empty lives are lonely, no matter how many friends one has or how many things we may have. Empty lives in the middle of paradise or utopia are still empty. In the garden of Eden many years ago, God created Eve as a "helpmate" for Adam. Together they filled each other's lives with love. Together they shared the life God had given them. Two people sharing—loving—to make both happy and fulfilled. Two people, a man and a woman, sharing life together. In many wedding ceremonies, the bride and groom each take a lighted candle and together light another, their wedding candle, two lives becoming one in fullness and love. They have taken vows to love, honor, cherish, and protect each other.

Lives that are filled with love are happier and healthier. Lives shared with love, where both are partners caring for and about the other's well-being. Lives where the other's dreams, goals and even shortcomings are respected. Christ taught us to love one another and pray for those who persecute us. Christ taught us many things about love. Yet we live in a world dominated by greed, selfishness, divisiveness, hate, and empty lives. Lives that may possess mountains of wealth or lives that may only have small hills of wealth, but lives that are still empty, still lacking in love, the only *thing* that can fill them.

In 1 Corinthians, Chapter 13 we read, "...and the greatest of these is love." Love that conquers all. Love, which rarely, if ever, can be explained, only felt. The reality of empty lives or empty boxes is no matter how well decorated with material goods or pretty paper and ribbon, they are still empty. To fill these lives, all that is needed is love—love of God, of friends, of family, of spouse, of children. Love that is never loud, unlike hate, which is never soft.

Empty lives, whether real or symbolic, need only love. Love that does more than anything else. Love that fills the empty box or the empty life.

—hd

How do we or can we help to fill empty lives of those around us?

Think About It

Life goes on and at times when things go wrong,
as they will; we all feel cheated–
but think about it. Were we?

Were we promised a carefree, happy,
healthy life here on earth?
Think about it.

Life is often hard,
life is often cruel,
life is often heartaches,
life is often painful,
life is often sickness.

Just what *were* we promised?

Think about it!

Source: Herbert Dettmer

The reality of life often hits us hard and never at a convenient time. While we strive to be happy, healthy, and successful in our daily living, reality seems to be working against us. We complain, criticize, and sometimes sue others over what has happened to us. "We don't deserve this," we say. We need or want _____, because we deserve it. Do we? Who said we can have it all? That we *deserve* it all?

What was promised by the One who never fails to deliver? Were we promised a happy, healthy, carefree, and stress-free life? Were we promised a life without problems? Were we promised an easy life without cruelty, heartache, pain, and illness?

We were given life and a rule book, The Holy Bible. How we live our lives, and how we act and react to the realities of our life—heartache, disappointment, success, illness, and all the other realities of life—is how we will be judged when our day comes to meet our maker at the gates of heaven.

Deep down inside each one of us is the answer. When the reality of life turns our lives upside down, just think about it. When life hurts us, whether physically or otherwise, just think. When our lives are headed in a way we don't want, perhaps even beyond our control, think, just *what* were we promised?

—hd

How does the *reality* of life affect our well-planned goals in life?

Which Is Me?

Within my earthly temple, there is a crowd.
There's one of us who is humble and one who is proud.

There's one who is heartbroken for all his sins, and one who is unrepentant; he just sits and grins.

There's one who loves his neighbor as himself, and one who cares naught, but for fame and self.

From such corroding care, I should be free, if once I could determine, which is me?

Source: H. D. Fish

God has given each of us certain talents, skills, and interests. He has also given us the ability to think and to reason. This ability permits us to make the decisions about every facet of our lives. (It also sets us apart from all other living things.)

Regardless of our profession or education or under-standing of the many complexities of our world, there are many simple choices we can make. The basic dif-ference between right and wrong may seem easy to understand. Yet to follow our beliefs in a stress-filled, pressure-filled world where one must always win in order to succeed or to just stay even, it may be difficult to choose. To swallow our pride and be humble may cost us the sale or even the job. Just how right do we have to be?

When we err, sin, do we try to justify our actions or inactions? "I had to do that or lose out to the com-petition." Repentance or justification, who will lose in the end?

With so many in need of the basic necessities of life or just a friendly shoulder to cry on, how do we reach out? And why? "Is it deductible?" we often ask as we write a check. Is this the reason to donate money to a worthy cause? Or could we add a "0," to really help?

When trouble or heartache strikes and money won't solve the problem, are we too busy to listen to a friend? Or offer our shoulder? Do we say, "That's too bad about so and so, but I have my own life to live?"

Which is me? One who thinks about our neighbors or who one thinks only of himself?

Which is me? One who is sorry and repentant for his sins or one who just grins?

Within each of us we can find the answer.

Within each of us we know which and what is right.

Within each of us, which is you? Which is me?

—hd

Others

There is good and not so good in each one of us. We all have strong points and weak points. What we do with these, how we develop them, is who we are.

Smiles and Trouble

Smiles

Smiles cost nothing, they are catching, and a smile can give so much hope.

You may help another brother, if you laugh instead of mope.

In the face that's always smiling, beauty shines out from the soul.

Smile and help the one who's trying with all his might to reach a goal.

When with life you get so tired, and your lot looks almost black.

Don't despair, pull up the corners of your mouth into a pack of wrinkles that will ripple into smiles.

And forget the many worries that have gathered into trials, use your laughter as you travel.

For a smile just grows and grows, and a smile will make one forget his woes.

You can spread a little sunshine, in a smile you but impart.

So reflect a smile upon your face, and laughter in your heart.

Source: H. D. Fish

Trouble

If your life is full of trouble, and you feel you've lost the game,

Don't forget the other fellow may have worries just the same.

Try and look a little pleasant, as the goal you aim to win.

For there's always grit and courage, in the folks who laugh and sing.

You are not the only fellow who is saddened by despair;

There are others by the dozens who have troubles hard to bear.

So be brave and fight harder; learn to bear the cross and grin,

and be ready to grip tighter, for a fighter can but win.

Source: H. D. Fish

Life can be full of bliss and happiness, hard work and play. Life can also give us problems, sometimes many problems. We plan our education and careers carefully. But in spite of our plans, problems arise through no fault of our own. Competition is keen, everyone is trying to reach their goal, but not everyone can. Sometimes, maybe often, we feel all hope is lost.

When trouble comes, it never makes an appointment. It seems to always arrive at the least convenient time. The car breaks down on an important trip (maybe our vacation). The furnace quits during the coldest week in January. Just before the family picture is to be taken, your teenage daughter gets a pimple. Is all lost? To your teen, it may be the end of the world. To the teen who just learned his parents are getting a divorce, a pimple may seem like a blessing. To the family whose house burned, a furnace that just quit is a minor inconvenience. But to the young widow with a small child, the burned house may pale in comparison, to a car breaking down, a furnace quitting, a pimple, or a house fire, or—anything.

Everyone has problems. Trouble finds us no matter where we live, how much money we have, or how little. Problems and troubles are all around us, big ones and little ones. Sometimes they are self-inflicted by poor planning or lack of planning. Other times they come to us by chance through no fault of our own.

How we handle these problems says much about us. Do we "take it in stride," or do we whine and cry? Do we try to overcome the troubles that affect us? Or do we blame someone else? Keeping a positive attitude and smile on our face can help us overcome whatever problems we face. The important thing is to keep trying. Try and try again. "Quitters never win and winners never quit" is an expression often used in sports. It is good advice in any situation. Though some problems are seemingly insurmountable, most can be overcome with effort—effort, hard work, and a positive attitude.

Nothing positive ever happened by a negative attitude. The courage to face our problems and troubles comes from within each of us.

In recent years, the yellow smiley face has been seen almost everywhere in one way or another, reminding everyone to be happy and pleasant. With life as complex and confusing as it is today, a smile is about the only way to maintain one's sanity. How much more pleasant and enjoyable life would be if people would smile and laugh more. Even with the problems and trouble we have. Confrontation seems to be the norm, and many people try to be in control of everything, which makes any communication or activity between them even more stressful and often impossible.

Smiles and troubles; positive and negative feelings. Courage is positive. Despair is negative. The despair we feel is not easily overcome. It can and will defeat us, but only if we let it. We must stand up to our problems courageously and bravely and challenge them, fight them. One way is to smile.

Try and try again, never quit. As we work and fight to solve our problems, keeping a grin on our face we will overcome anything. Remembering always the ultimate victory symbolized by the empty tomb.

—hd

How can we smile when faced with problems (troubles)? Will it help get through these times?

Builders

We are builders, you and I,
Each with a certain task to do,
And as the days go swiftly by,
We build awhile, then we are three.

Our bricks are made of little deeds,
The kindly word, the cheerful smile,
A helping hand for those in need,
And time to visit the sick awhile.

The mortar must be very strong,
To cement these all together,
So we are held by friendships long,
In fair or stormy weather.

The Golden Rule we measure by
So our building will be straight and true,
Do unto others we should try,
As we would have them do.

So the Great Architect, by and by,
may inspect and approve our work.

Source: H. D. Fish

Is this about working together in life, learning to set a good example, team work with our parents and teachers as we grow to be adults, team work with our coworkers and supervisors as we live in the real world?

Living our lives as we learned in Sunday school as little children, living our lives as Christ taught us, doing more, growing, and spreading the Word of God to others by our example. Sometimes a small deed, a kind word, is all that is needed. Lead and teach by our example, as Christ is our example.

In good times and bad, our friendships, our team, will cement all our deeds, so all can see God's way is the *only* way. Following the golden rule will make our building strong. So when our creator, the Great Architect, sees our work—the good we've done in our life—He will approve.

—hd

Building our lives involves many tasks. Education is one of them. Experience and common sense are two others. We learn from experience, and common sense, what about them?

This Old World

It's a wicked old world, I've you say,
a wicked old world and I will agree.
That trouble and sorrow block the way,
and sunshine is often hard to see.
It's a wicked old world, but tell me, son,
are you trying to make it a better one?

Are you adding your sigh to the mournful chant,
or are you lifting a song of cheer?
Are you lending your voice to the tone of can't,
or are you scattering sunshine here?
It's a wicked old world—but the work you've done,
has it helped to make it a better one?

Did the word you spoke tend to stop the tears?
Did your hand raise someone who has chanced
to fall?
Did the hope you preached put an end to fears?
Did you rush aid when you heard the call?
It's a wicked old world, Alas! my son,
but have you made it a better one?

Source: H. D. Fish

Yes, it is a wicked old world out there. We've heard the news reports. We've read about the current events of the world. Be it war, famine, earthquake, tsunami, or any of the crimes people commit, what have we done to make the world a better place? Send a check to the various relief organizations? When the towers of the World Trade Center fell on September 11, 2001, rescue workers rushed to New York from all over our country. But what did you do? When Katrina and Rita devastated the gulf coast in 2005 and the Haiti earthquake in 2010, the same thing happened. What did *you* do? It's a wicked old world. Man-made and natural disasters don't help, but have you done anything to help make it better? Or do we sit watching the events unfold on TV, perhaps silently thanking God we don't live there? Have we actually *done* something to help?

Have we actually done something to help in our local community? Something little, yet something positive? Helping out in major disasters and tragedies, no matter how we do it, is vitally important and necessary. But in everyday life there are needs as well. It's a wicked old world—next door, across the country, and across the oceans—what have you done to make it a better one?

—hd

Just what makes a "better" world? Do we setout to change everything to our liking without thinking of *Others*? Or is it better just to set a positive example with how we live?

The Unfulfilled Dream

The unfulfilled dream.
The love turned aside,
the hurt and the anger,
the wounded pride.

Oh Lord, make us stop and please make
us see the way that you planned it,
and meant it to be.

Source: Bonnie J. O'Brien

How often have we lost sight of the way of our Lord? How often have we broken the heart of someone we love? While growing up, adolescent romances are constantly developing and dissolving. Both people are hurt by the love turned aside. As adults too, relationships and marriages are broken up by love turned aside. There is anger and hurt no matter who is at fault. Usually both people involved are at least partly at fault. Friendships too are affected by unfulfilled dreams.

How many times have we lost sight of the way of our Lord? Wounded pride and hurt feelings and selfishness in relationships are not what Jesus taught us.

Yet, we as Christians seem to do things contrary to His teachings. Why? Because we're human? Probably, but also because we don't follow in His footsteps as carefully as we could—as carefully as we *should*.

"Oh Lord, make us stop and please make us see the way that you planned it, and meant it to be."

—hd

How easy it is to be thought*less* and how hard it is to be thought*ful*. Both in our youth and as adults.

The Beatitudes–
Matthew 5: 1-12

And seeing the multitudes, He went up into the mountain: and when He had sat down, His disciples came to Him and He opened His mouth and taught them saying,

Blessed are the poor in spirit; for theirs is the kingdom of Heaven.

Blessed are they that mourn; for they should be comforted.

Blessed are the meek; for they shall inherit the earth.

Blessed are they that hunger and thirst after righteousness; for they shall be filled.

Blessed are the merciful; for they shall obtain mercy.

Blessed are the pure in heart; for they shall see God.

Blessed are the peacemakers; for they shall be called the sons of God.

Blessed are they that have been persecuted for righteousness' sake; for theirs is the kingdom of Heaven.

Blessed are ye when men shall reproach you and persecute you, and say all manner of evil against you falsely, for my sake.

Rejoice and be exceedingly glad; for great is your reward in Heaven; for so persecuted they the prophets that were before you.

Source: H. D. Fish's personal Bible

The Beatitudes are one of the most easily recognized of all the teachings of Jesus. The multitudes, the followers of Jesus, gathered to hear His words. How many were there? The exact number is not important, only that there was a large crowd eagerly waiting to hear Him. Notice that Jesus talked only of those who are in need of something, those who are humble. Nothing was said about the rich, the proud, or those who felt their life didn't need anything that was not materially or position enriching.

Who are:

The poor in spirit? Those who need more self-esteem and self-confidence, not the proud, the arrogant, the egotistical.

They that mourn? Not just those who have lost a loved one in death, but also those who mourn their sins and seek forgiveness.

The meek? Followers who truly humble themselves before God.

They that hunger and thirst? Are the ones who are trying to learn everything about God and Jesus to live their life accordingly.

The merciful? Who live quiet and humble lives, forgiving others for their sins and show compassion for others—who think of others not themselves.

The pure in heart? People who try to live as Christ teaches and, though not sinless, have a closer understanding than most of us.

The peacemakers? Work for a peaceful world; missionaries, soldiers, clergy, anyone who works to end ignorance, war, and famine and seeks to spread the word of God.

The persecuted? Anyone who believes and follows the teachings of Jesus and is physically, mentally, or emotionally harmed or injured because of those beliefs.

Christ was talking to and about all of us who truly believe and follow Him. The multitudes today might include those who are seeking a job, a place to live, warm clothing, health care, or any of the numerous modern needs we as a society are striving to obtain.

Reading the Beatitudes should comfort us and show us that Jesus cared about those on that mountain just as He cares about us on our mountain.

—hd

Seriously think about each of these. In today's world, what would Jesus have said?

The Lord's Prayer

Our Father, which art in Heaven,

Hallowed be Thy name.

Thy kingdom come, Thy will be done,

in Earth, as it is in Heaven.

Give us this day, our daily bread,

And forgive us our debts, as we

have forgiven our debtors.

And lead us not into temptation,

but deliver us from evil.

For Thine is the kingdom,

and the Power and the Glory,

forever.

Amen

Source: Matthew 6: 9-14, King James Version
of the Holy Bible

The Lord's Prayer, so familiar we recite it often without even thinking. We recite it and never, or rarely, think about what it means or says.

Our Father, which art in Heaven...

God Almighty, creator of the universe, the stars, the sun, planets, and the moon; God, our heavenly Father who sees all, hears all, and knows all; God, who knows when a sparrow falls and who knows the suffering of the hungry and the homeless; God, who Christ prayed to, who gave Moses the law, who each of us have our own concept of who or what God is; God, our Father, who lives in the heavens and in the hearts of each one of us. Heaven, "up there," we tell our children because we don't really know where it is. Heaven, "Where Grandpa and Aunt Sophie went when they died to be with God and Jesus," we tell our children. Heaven, wherever it is, God is there, yet He lives in each one of us.

Hallowed be thy name...

Hallowed or holy. The thesaurus lists many words that can be used to describe "holy." God our Creator, His name is sacred, sacrosanct, and many, many others. What do these mean? Mere human words cannot adequately describe the meaning of holy or hallowed. We must accept God as the ultimate power. The most high being or spirit, or however we try to describe Him.

Thy kingdom come, Thy will be done...

God's kingdom, the promise referred to often in the Holy Bible, will come to earth. When? How? Why? We can only guess. When? When God is ready, or perhaps when in His eyes we, His people, deserve it. Whenever His kingdom comes, will any of us be ready? Or will it arrive at the most inconvenient time for us? God's will, not ours. God rules the heaven and the earth. His power vastly exceeds anything we humans could dream of creating. Not even the combination of all the most powerful nuclear warheads came close to the awesome power of God. Massive earthquakes, hurricanes, and volcanoes destroy more than any nuclear device. For example, the tsunami of December 2004, hurricanes Katrina and Rita in 2005, and the earthquake in Pakistan in 2005, in Haiti in 2010, the earthquake, tsunami, and nuclear plant meltdown in Japan in 2011. Yet the power of God created the bumblebee and hummingbird, which scientists and biologists say should not, cannot fly. God's will, God's power, God's way.

In earth as it is in heaven...

While God rules in heaven, we think we can rule our lives, our communities, and our nation. Our very lives depend on God. Our nation's laws and the Bill of Rights mirror the Ten Commandments. Stealing, killing, even telling a lie are violations of God's laws and man's. Stealing and killing are easy to see, but lying? Compare perjury and bearing false witness. God's will and kingdom in time, God's time will prevail on earth as it does in heaven.

Give us this day, our daily bread...

God gave us life. He blessed our parents with each of us and provides for our daily needs, our daily nourishment. We only need to make the effort and look for what He provides. But God won't "spoon feed" us; we need to feed ourselves. But He provides for *all* our needs, not just the food for our bodies, the food for our minds, and the food for our spirit. The education we need to make a living, the understanding we need to live our lives according to His Word, and, most important, the love we need to live.

And forgive us our debts, as we forgive our debtors...

God created us in His image, but He didn't create us perfect. We are all born into sin, debt. Some Bibles call it trespasses, meaning against. Either way we are all sinners. We live, work, and play, and in doing so, no matter how careful we are, we will sin. God forgives us, but only if we ask His forgiveness. Just as we should forgive those who sin against us. Just as Jesus did on the cross, "Father forgive them..." A little tolerance, understanding, and forgiveness for others' sins will make us all better people. Remember, "Do unto others..."

And lead us not unto temptation, but deliver us from evil...

The devil is always there to tempt us with the easy way, the fun way, the way we may want to go, but not the way God commands us. While the easy and fun way may not always be wrong, we need to be careful we don't cross that invisible line dividing God's way from the other way. Temptation itself is not a sin, but giving in to it is. We ask God to lead us away from the temptations of the devil and deliver us from his evil ways.

For Thine is the Kingdom and the Power and the Glory, forever.

The kingdom, power, and glory all belong to God our Creator. "This is our Father's World" is a popular hymn in many churches. How true. God created the universe, the heavens, and the earth, His earth. We only live here because He created us and put us here. Everything that happens, God knows. From the smallest living organism, to the massive sequoia, God knows, cares, and loves. It's up to us to live according to His rules, His commandments, and if we don't, God is the final judge, and there is no court of appeals at the gates of heaven.

—hd

Instead of just *saying* the words, think about each word and phrase and what they mean.

An Old Story

One hot summer day a young boy and an old man were walking together on a beach. Every time they saw a starfish on the sand, the young boy would pick it up and throw it back into the sea. After a while the old man asked the boy, "Why are you doing that?"

And the boy said, "If a starfish is out of the water too long, it will shrivel up and die."

The old man replied, "That's right, but there are thousands of miles of beaches and millions of starfish. What difference can you make in all of that?"

The young but very wise boy turned to the old man and said, "It makes a difference to this one," as he threw another starfish into the sea.

Source: Unknown

No matter how small the deed, do something positive, and it will make a difference to someone. Our world is big with "thousands of miles of beaches and millions of starfish," but every small and kind deed makes a difference to someone. Even just smiling to a stranger or holding the door for someone, they will remember. Maybe not you, but that someone out there cared enough to be kind. It might make a big difference in their day. Remember, any journey begins with just one step.

Big things are built with little things. A better, happier, more peaceful world is built by everyone doing the little things, the smile, a kind word, holding the door, or throwing the starfish back into the sea.

—hd

What difference have we made by even the smallest, seemingly most insignificant deed?

I Asked the Lord

I asked the Lord, "How much do you love me?"

He said, "This much." Then He stretched out His arms...and died.

Source: Unknown

"What a friend we have in Jesus" is a popular hymn in many churches. Little children in Sunday school, learn "Jesus loves me this I know..." In the Gospel of John, Chapter 15, verse 13, we read, "Greater love has no man than this; that he lay down his life for his friends."

Is there *anything* else to say?

—hd

"Greater love has no man than this..." Seriously think about the significance of this.

Thoughts of a Soldier at Christmas

Far from home in some distant land, the dark of night descended. A lonely soldier stood at his post watching, listening. A light snow was falling; it was the Sunday before Christmas. The quiet was as intense as the cold. The lonely soldier thought of the carol "Silent Night." "Silent Night, Holy Night," the familiar words came forth soundlessly from his lips, "All is calm, all is bright." He studied the surrounding area. Nothing moved, and the soft falling snow reminded him of Christmases of past years. Last minute shopping, wrapping presents, and preparing for the celebration of the birth of baby Jesus, the prince of peace.

Peace, that ever-elusive dream. Peace, more than the absence of war. Peace, what every minister preaches about. Peace, the *dream* of every soldier.

Christmas carols sang of the joy of the season. Christmas cards, he recalled, had messages of peace, love, joy, and happiness. Yet here he stood, rifle in hand, ready to fight, to kill, and possibly to die. From the deep recesses of his memories he heard, "Let there be peace on earth, and let it begin with me..." Suddenly, despite the snow and cold, the soldier felt an inner warmth. A warmth he'd never felt before. Was it possible? Could it really be? His mind worked hard trying to remember, as he gazed over the snow-covered landscape in that faraway land. Somewhere in his Bible he'd read, long ago, "Blessed are the Peacemakers." He couldn't remember the rest of the verse, but yes, *he* was a *peacemaker*. Standing guard, he was doing his job, maintaining peace in a troubled world, a world full of hate and violence. A world where at anytime he could be called on to fight, to kill, and possibly to *die* for the cause of peace.

"Blessed are the Peacemakers..." He felt better, warmer. No longer was he alone and afraid, for he was indeed blessed. The words of the carol came back. "Let there be peace on earth, and let it begin with me..."

He changed some the words as he quietly hummed the familiar tune while watching and listening.

> For I am a *Soldier*,
> and I am a *fighter*,
> and I *know* what war is like.
> Let there be Peace on earth,
> and let it begin with me.

Yes, "Blessed are the Peacemakers." Blessed are the soldiers who stand guard in every land, ready to defend freedom and bring peace to this troubled world. Blessed *indeed* are the soldiers, the sailors, the marines, the airmen, and the coast guardsmen. All who serve and have served in uniform, for they truly are the peacemakers. Perhaps more so than anyone, for they are the ones who know, *really know*, what the absence of peace *really* means.

As we celebrate the birth of our Savior, the prince of peace, let us be like that lonely soldier on guard duty, ever watchful, always listening, aware of even that little thought or deed that may help to bring peace to our trouble world. For Jesus taught us...

"Blessed are the Peacemakers, for they shall be called the children of God."

Source: Herbert Dettmer, US Army Veteran.

I wrote this during the Bosnia and Kosovo "peacekeeping" missions. How might this apply to everyday civilian life?

'Twas the Week before...
I Have to Make a List!

Oh my goodness, Thanksgiving is only five days away! There is so much to do. I know, I'll make a list. I have to clean the house, scrub the floor, wash windows, buy groceries, bake the pies, iron the tablecloth, make the centerpiece...

What did you say? Christmas is only thirty-seven days away? There is so much to do. I know, I'll make another list. I have to shop, shop, shop, write the cards, buy stamps, decorate the house, put up the tree, wrap the presents, clean the house, go to school concerts, change the sheets—company is coming...

What do you mean, who do I think I am? I am a wife and mother, I have to do all these thing; it's expected of me. Who else will do it? Sure, my husband and children will help, but they don't know how much there is to do. Never enough time. Never!

Don't we know the meaning of Thanksgiving? Sure, when the dishes are done and the relatives have gone home, I'm thankful to kick off my shoes, get the kids to bed, and fall asleep on the couch.

Does my family celebrate the birth of Jesus at Christmas? Sure we do. We go to church, exchange presents, and you should see the beautiful manger scene we have. It cost a bundle, but it sure looks nice on the mantle. There's more to these holidays, you say?

What more can there be? Don't knock myself out to get ready? But...but...if I have to make a list, you say, make one that tells me of all the things I have to be thankful for. Okay, here it is:

My wonderful, loving husband of many years.

My healthy, normal, beautiful children.

My parents and in-laws who are always there for love and guidance.

My health and the health of my husband.

My cozy, safe home.

The jobs my husband and I have.

All our dear and faithful friends.

That our community is safe from violence.

That we have food on our table and warm clothes for the winter.

I'm beginning to see what you mean. Thanksgiving is more than eating turkey and entertaining relatives. And Christmas is more than presents and fussing. Christmas is the birthday of our Lord, Jesus Christ. We sing the carols in church, but do we listen, *really* listen to the words?

This mother, this wife, is going to make a new list, a short one, just one item, reflecting: "Jesus is the reason for the season."

Source: Rebecca Dettmer

Step back from the business that clouds the seasons. Be organized, yes, but we must not forget the purpose of our business. We must continually count and be thankful for our blessings both large and small. Enjoy the holidays, make lists for comfort, but most of all, we should never forget the meaning of the holiday.

Who Am I? Who Are You?

Beyond names, beyond race and ethnic background, beyond economic position, who are we? Even beyond our unique and individual personalities, just who are we?

We are creatures of the ever-living, ever-loving God. No matter what we do, how we think, or what we say, God created us. No matter how we rationalize, justify, or otherwise try to explain our existence, God created us. We are His. He gave us life and a place to live: planet earth. God gave us dominion over all that grows and lives on, in, and under our home. He gave us everything we have or ever will have. He even gave us a Savior who died on the cross for *our* sins. Why? Simply because He loves us. And what does God ask in return? Only that we love Him and obey His laws and Commandments.

Who am I? Who are you? We are God's children. But are we good children? Do we obey the laws and Commandments He gave us? Or do we travel through life according to our own wants and desires? Our own agenda and priorities? Do we tell little lies to protect ourselves and enhance our position? Do we exaggerate so we feel better about what we did? Or to look good in the eyes of our peers? Do we make excuses for what we failed to do? Perhaps we blame others for our mistakes or take credit for their ideas? Right or wrong, good or bad, our society has grown to accept these falsehoods and even expect them. But the Bible says, "Thou shalt not bear false witness against thy neighbor." Neighbor being not only the people who live next door but anyone we have contact with in our daily lives. Remember the story of the Good Samaritan?

Who am I? Who are you? While we run through our lives protecting ourselves with these little lies, making excuses and exaggerating for our benefit, we are learning how easy it is to get away with it. At the same time unconsciously or subconsciously, we are preparing our minds to move to the big time. With bigger lies and falsehoods, we are hoping for bigger earthly rewards. Yet we still profess a belief in God, Jesus, and the Ten Commandments. Try as we might to follow and obey God's laws, the short-term *tangible* rewards and benefits are more enticing than the intangible and unknown eternal rewards and benefits of life with God our Father in heaven.

Who am I? Who are you? We know what to do, but our priorities are out of sync. We are more concerned about making the house payment and the car payment than we are with the fact we have a house and car, food on the table, and our health. Are we more concerned about being cool and accepted, even admired by our friends and peers than we are with the fact that Jesus is a friend to all? He loves us and His Father in heaven loves us.

Who am I? Who are you? We are believers in God and followers of Jesus Christ. At least we claim we are. We do when all else fails. We do in times of crisis and tragedy. We go to church, sing the hymns, listen to the sermon, write a check for the offering, and visit with our friends after the service. Then go to a football or baseball game and swear at the referees or umpires and probably the players too. Maybe we go to work, shopping at the mall, perhaps a picnic, or just go home and watch TV, forgetting completely that the Sabbath should be "kept holy." Only when confronted with a crisis, a tragedy, or when we really want something, do we turn to God in prayer. "It's Sunday, time to go to church." Isn't what Jesus taught us? Being part-time or occasional Christians only makes us hypocrites.

Who am I? Who are *you?* We are God's children, the sheep of His pasture. What is the symbolism of being His sheep? Or has symbolism been lost in our modern society? Are we too concerned with our image and what others think of us that we forget, or worse ignore the fact we are the sheep of the Good Shepherd? Are we trying too hard to impress our peers? With our vast and continuing education, have we become so smart we don't need God? We can take care of ourselves, and the government can take care of those who can't or won't take care of themselves. So now we can enjoy life, play golf, take our boat out on the lake, or whatever leisure activity we choose. We can attend to our careers, our pleasures, our financial independence, and we retire in style. The sheep may follow the shepherd to fresh grazing areas, but we've got it all together, or so we think. What about our spiritual needs? We've been so busy; have we neglected them? Have we been *honest* and *sin-*

cere about our beliefs? For when that time comes, and we leave this earthly life, will it matter what and how much our stock portfolio contained? Or our pension plans? Will it matter if our earthly bodies are in top physical condition? When we stand before God our creator seeking entrance into life eternal, God alone will judge us. He will judge us not for how much we accumulated in worldly wealth, but how we lived, how we dealt with the challenges of life, and what we did with our wealth; what we did and what we failed or neglected to do.

Who am I? Who are you? Who are we? What are we? With everything else we are, what should describe us most? Best? We are sinners! We have a loving and forgiving creator who has given us a Savior who died on the cross for all the sins of all people in the world.

Who am I? Who are you? Beyond our names, ethnic backgrounds, financial positions, even beyond our personalities, we are God's children, the sheep of His pasture. We can obey His rules and laws, or not. That is our choice. We can follow Jesus Christ our Savior, or not, that too is our choice. God's laws and the teachings of Jesus are clear. Understanding them is not hard. Following and obeying them does take effort, and that effort is well worth the rewards, whatever they are, that await us.

Who am I? Who are you? We are God's children. We can make our friends think we are with it or cool. We can even fool strangers, but God knows what we do and how we live. What matters most? What our friends think? Or God?

Who am I? Who are you?

Source: Herbert Dettmer.

We are human and we make mistakes. What a shame
we do not give our Maker the same love and attention
everyday that we do in times of trouble.

Count Your Blessings

Count your blessings instead of your crosses.

Count your gains instead of your losses.

Count your joys instead of your woes.

Count your friends instead of your foes.

Count your smiles instead of your tears.

Count your courage instead of your fears.

Count your full years instead of your lean.

Count your kind deeds instead of your mean.

Count your health instead of your wealth.

And most of all—count on God, instead of yourself.

Source: Unknown

Try to list your non-material blessings.

Turn it Over

We pray to God, asking for forgiveness of our sins, understanding in our troubles, and maybe even to win the lottery.

We pray to God, thanking Him for our blessings, our health, our comfortable homes, our families, friends, and church.

We pray to God, praising Him and worshipping Him, but when God speaks to us, do we listen?

A dear lady I know has said many times, "Turn it over." Turn it over to God, no matter what "it" is, a problem, a crisis, or asking guidance.

Turn it over to Him, who has created us and who loves us in spite of our numerous shortcomings. How often have we "turned over" a problem to God, only to be disappointed that the problem wasn't solved the way *we* wanted it solved? Or maybe the problem wasn't solved at all. (Maybe it was, but we just didn't accept the solution.) What did we ask for? A promotion? To win the *big* game? The lottery? None of which we received.

Did we ask for His healing hand for a loved one's illness only to have our loved one pass away? Were we upset or angry at God because of this? Does God hear these prayers? Or is He too busy listening to everyone's requests and some get lost in the shuffle? No! God does hear all our prayers, even the selfish ones. But who has the final say on anything? Us? Or God? We say, "Thy will be done," but do we really mean it? Or is it when we want something we can't get on our own that we seek divine assistance? Yes, God answers our prayers, but not always in the way *we* want them answered. That loved one who passed away was healed. In our sorrow we just didn't realize that death is a form of healing.

When we turn it over, do we hold on to it just a little? Maybe so we don't completely lose control of our lives? If so, we really haven't turned it over, have we? Our faith in God isn't quite strong enough to let go completely. How many times have we said, "God, if you give me _____, I will do _____?" And somehow we have conveniently forgotten our part of the bargain. (Not that we *really* can make a bargain with God.) Next time we decide to turn it over, let all of us do so completely then butt out. Perhaps we should think, turn it over, and let go; let God take care of it. Who better to trust? Who better to invite into our lives? Who else will *unselfishly* take care of us?

Source: Herbert Dettmer.

Why is it we wait to do this, "when everything else fails"?

'Twas the Night Before (Number 2)

'Twas the night before Christmas; he lived all alone,

In a one bedroom house made of plaster and stone.

I had come down the chimney with presents to give

And to see just who in this home did live.

I looked all about; a strange sight I did see,

No tinsel, no presents, not even a tree.

No stocking by mantle, just boots filled with sand,

On the wall hung pictures of far distant lands

With medals and badges, awards of all kinds.

A sober thought came through my mind.

For this house was different, it was dark and dreary.

I found the home of a soldier, once I could see clearly.

The soldier lay sleeping, silent, alone,

Curled up on the floor, in this one bedroom home.

The face was so gentle, the room in such disorder,

Not how I pictured a United States soldier.

Was this the hero of whom I just read?

Curled up on a poncho, the floor for a bed?

I realized the families that I saw this night,

Owed their lives to these soldiers, who were willing
to fight.

Soon round the world, the children would play,

And grown-ups would celebrate a bright Christmas
Day.

They all enjoyed freedom each month of the year

Because of the soldiers, like the one lying here.

I couldn't help wonder how many lay alone

On a cold Christmas Eve in a land far from home.

The very thought brought a tear to my eye.

I dropped to my knees and started to cry.

The soldier awakened, and I heard a rough voice:

"Santa, don't cry. This life is my choice.

I fight for freedom; I don't ask for more.

My life is my God, my country, my Corps."

The soldier rolled over and drifted to sleep.

I couldn't control it, I continued to weep.

I kept watch for hours, so silent and still,

And we both shivered from the cold night's chill.

I didn't want to leave on that cold, dark night

This guardian of honor so willing to fight.

The soldier rolled over, with a voice soft and pure,

Whispered, "Carry on, Santa, it's Christmas Day,
all is secure."

One look at my watch, and I knew he was right,

"Merry Christmas, my friend, and to all a good
night."

Source: Written by an unknown US Marine, stationed in Okinawa, Japan, Christmas 2000. Found on the Internet 12-12-2000.

My God, my country, my corps. This marine has his priorities in order. Far from home, with every reason to be sad and alone, the author of this poem gives us the *real* picture of what it is like to be serving our nation in the military. Without them and their service, our freedoms would be in great danger. Without all the veterans, our nation would not be as we know it today. During the holidays especially, but all during the year, we should remember all Americans serving in the US Armed Forces. As Herbert Fish wrote in his prayer at the beginning of this book—

> Others, Lord, yes others,
> let this my motto be,
> help me live for others,
> that I may live like Thee.

Serving *others* is what our military people do. Serving for, fighting for, and sometimes even *dying* for our freedom, the freedom of and for *others*.

—hd

Next holiday season, say an extra prayer for our servicemen and women. Better yet, let's not wait for the holidays.

Lost? Or Found!

We have all lost something sometime in our busy lives, a good pen, a screwdriver, maybe a watch, perhaps a ring or other piece of jewelry. It can be disappointing at the least and heartbreaking or even tragic at the worst if the item lost was of value. Especially if it was of *real* value, either monetary or sentimental.

Losing a loved one to death is probably the biggest loss anyone can experience. It doesn't matter what the cause of death is, the loss is no less a loss. There is a story about a woman whose son died. He was a very popular young man. People sought him out every day, treated him like a real hero, although there were some who didn't like him. But most people who heard him speak listened intently and soon believed he was like no one else. They followed him everywhere. But as any popular person soon learns, there are those who don't like popular people. Maybe they feel threatened by them or they are just jealous. They will do anything to discredit the popular one, even if it means ruining their reputation, causing bodily harm, or worse, causing their death. The news is full of stories like this. Check with any politician, movie star, or other celebrity.

This woman lost her son to a handful of jealous and dangerous community leaders. They charged with serious crimes he didn't really commit. Tried him in their court and convicted him. He was sentenced to death, executed, then buried. The mother was devastated. Her son's friends tried to console her with little success. Shortly after he was buried, the mother, with a couple of her friends, went to his grave hoping to ease the sorrow at this tragic loss. But when they arrived, they saw the grave had been opened and her son's body was gone. First she lost her son to death, then her son's body somehow was lost. There was nothing for her now, not even a grave.

That's not the end of the story. This woman, Mary was her name, soon learned her son, though He had indeed died, had overcome that tragedy. He fulfilled the prophesy stated long before.

Whoever believes in the ultimate victory symbolized by the empty tomb and Easter will never be *lost*. Jesus, Mary's son, paid the price for all of us. Those who have *found* Him, and follow Him, need only remember what He taught us.

Source: Herbert Dettmer.

Are we still *lost*? Or have we *found* the answer.

The Color Red

The color red, what does it mean to you?

Roses are red; violets are blue...
Stop signs are red.
Many warning signs are red.
Red sky in the morning, sailors take warning.
Shiny red apples.
Juicy red tomatoes.
Teachers often grade with a red pen or pencil,
So their marks will stand out.
Red is often used to decorate for the same reason.
How about a shiny new red car?
Better yet, a red 1957 Thunderbird convertible.
Or for you Chevy lovers, a red '57 Corvette.
Pentecost, the birthday of the church, is symbol-
ized by red.
Red is the color of romance.
A pretty, red dress with red unmentionables.
Red means anger.
Red, white, and blue, the colors of our nation's flag.
Christmas colors are red and green.
So are traffic lights.

Peace is symbolized by the color white.

When danger threatens, the military goes on *Red Alert*.

War is symbolized by the color red. Perhaps because of the blood spilled on the battlefield. Which means red stands for pain, suffering and death.

The same pain, suffering and death, which occurred at Calvary.

So does red stand for death? Or... does it stand for—Life?

Jesus suffered and died for our sins, and we use the cup at communion to seek forgiveness.

Forgiveness—Life—and the color red.

Source: Herbert Dettmer

What does the color red mean to you?

Bible Stories and War Stories

Ever since we can remember, we have heard stories: nursery rhymes, children's stories, and, in Sunday school, Bible stories. Noah and his Ark is one of the first stories I heard in my early Sunday school days. Others include Joseph and his beautiful coat, Adam and Eve, baby Moses, and David the shepherd boy. All helped to mold our minds and shape our lives. In addition to Bible stories we learned numerous Bible verses. "The Lord is my Shepherd," "In the beginning...God," "Do unto others...." The list goes on and on and includes, "Blessed are the Peacemakers..."

War stories and Bible stories—verses and phrases. Verses with special meanings we will never forget. Verses from Jesus like "Come, follow me," and phrases on a bumper sticker or a T-shirt—"All gave some ... some gave all."

Think about that as I relate a war story. Many years ago I saw a picture I will never forget. It was a picture of an event that occurred in February 1943. There were four men standing together. They were military men and were standing on the deck of a ship. Their ship had just been hit by torpedoes and was sinking. These men of different faiths had given their life jackets to four others so that they might live to fight the war and help bring peace to the world. These four men—

George Fox, a Methodist minister; Alexander Goode, a Jewish rabbi; Clark Poling, a Dutch reformed minister; and John Washington, a Roman Catholic priest; better known later as The Four Chaplains—were last seen standing together with their arms linked, praying as their ship, the *Dorchester*, sank in the cold dark waters of the North Atlantic. All gave some. . .some gave all.

There are many other stories of brave and courageous deeds. Bravery and courage, dedication and commitment to a just cause—the cause of *peace* and *freedom*.

This is a story of dedication and commitment. A young marine had almost completed his tour of duty in Southeast Asia when he decided to extend his tour. He wanted to make a difference, and he loved his country, his family, and his friends. This marine had been due to return home on January 28, 1968. By extending his tour of duty, he went the extra mile. As is written in the Gospel of Matthew, "whosoever shall compel thee to go with him one mile, go with him two." This marine was, as so many others were, dedicated and committed to the cause of *peace* and *freedom*. For those who may not remember, on January 31, 1968, just three days after this marine extended his tour, the Vietcong and North Vietnamese launched what became known as the Tet Offensive. That marine, that dedicated marine, who went the extra mile, gave his life on February 8. "Greater love has no man than this, that he lay down his life for his friends."

Jesus taught us about love—love for each other, for family, friends, and strangers—even for our enemies. (Pray for those who persecute you.) There is no better Bible story that shows love and compassion than the story of the Good Samaritan, where a man from one culture helps a severely injured man from another. A lesson we all should remember. A lesson repeated numerous times on the battlefield when wounded enemy soldiers are treated and cared for by American medics. Why? Because it is the right thing to do. This is what Christians believe *and* practice—even on the battlefield, *especially* on the battlefield. Retired marine Colonel Oliver North in a speech a couple of years ago described this best. He was in Iraq in 2003, shortly after we went in, and witnessed a navy medical corpsman in the heat of battle carrying two wounded marines to a waiting chopper. A Reuters news crew was at the edge of the road where the chopper had landed. The corpsman rushed back into heat of the battle, as the news crew filmed the action. The corpsman came back carrying yet another soldier, this time a wounded Iraqi soldier. A reporter called out to him, "Hey, mate, what did you do that for? Didn't you notice, that isn't a marine?" Remember, in 2003 we were fighting the Iraqis. The Corpsman glared at the reporter, then verbally responded, "Didn't you notice he is wounded? That's what we do, we're Americans." Yes, that's what we do. We're Americans. A perfect example of the Good Samaritan.

Sure there are stories, both proven and unproven, of atrocities and a blatant disregard for human life. It makes better news copy to report the negative. Yet the positive does exist. War brings out the worst of mankind but also the best. In Vietnam, Iraq, and Afghanistan and all the wars this nation has fought, there are stories and pictures of American troops giving food, water, and candy to numerous children in battle zones. These are rarely told by the mainstream media, but it happens more than we know. Friendships made in war often last far beyond the war's end. These friendships are often closer than any other...perhaps even marriage. Also, no one will ever know how many warriors have made battlefield commitments with God that even today, years and decades later, they have kept those commitments.

Here is another story. From the tenements of New York City, born out of wedlock, and raised by his grandmother, came a small, skinny kid. His friends said he was too scrawny to do much of anything. On August 6, 1950, his infantry unit was near Pusan, Korea. The enemy attacked, trapping his unit. Intense fighting followed. Then came the order to withdraw. But this scrawny kid held firm, and even though he was seriously wounded, he continued to fire his machine gun, slowing the enemy's advance, enabling his unit to withdraw. Then his gun fell silent. At Private William Thompson's funeral his minister said, "In the hour of need, he heard the cry of his country and gave all he had." Private Thompson went above and beyond the call of duty and received our nation's highest military award, the Congressional Medal of Honor. It was presented posthumously to his grandmother.

In all wars throughout history there are examples of these kinds of stories. Stories of great courage and bravery, of dedication and commitment. Not all result in death or the receiving of medals, but all do involve a risk. A risk everyone who serves in the military takes, a risk described by the Psalmist who wrote, "Yea though I walk through the valley of the shadow of death, I will fear no evil."

From David and Goliath and the Battle of Jericho and throughout history, warriors have worked for, fought for, and died for *peace* and *freedom*. From Lexington and Concord to Fort Sumpter, Gettysburg, and Appomattox—from San Juan Hill to the trenches of France and the beaches of Normandy—from Pearl Harbor and Okinawa to Inchon and the Frozen Chosin—from the Ia Trang Valley, Khe Sahn, and Hue to the deserts of Saudi Arabia and Kuwait—from the mountains and valleys of Bosnia and Kosovo and currently in Iraq and Afghanistan—Americans have lived and died fighting for *peace* and *freedom*. "Blessed are the Peacemakers." Making and maintaining peace is the main purpose of our military forces. Ask any one who has served if he or she would rather have war or peace.

Americans—men and women, rich and poor, from all ethnic and religious backgrounds—have given their lives for *peace* and *freedom*, for all Freedom-loving people. People like—

- The millions of Americans who have served our great nation in uniform,
- The four Chaplains on the *Dorchester*,
- That young Marine who went the extra mile,
- Private William Thompson in Korea,

- Herbert D. Fish, a close family friend who laid down his life on Okinawa,
- Daniel Pucci, a high school classmate of mine who gave his life in Vietnam.

They gave their lives for *peace* and *freedom*.

Military service in general and combat duty especially is a most unique experience. Where else in our society are men and women of different backgrounds, religious beliefs, and social standings thrown together, trained together, then put into some of the worst possible situations, under the worst possible conditions, and are *expected* to reach their objective—and they do! Where else might you find a black Catholic, a white Southern Baptist, an atheist, and a Jew huddled together in a foxhole or bunker, depending on each other for their very lives? How many soldiers during a lull on the battlefield read their pocket Bibles, often to each other? And how many tears are shed when a buddy is KIA—killed in action? These are the war stories people rarely hear, but *these*, my friends, these are the *real* war stories.

Bible stories and war stories—verses and phrases.

"All gave some...some gave all."

"Greater love has no man than this, that he lay down his life for his friends."

"And whosoever shall compel thee to go with him one mile, go with him two."

"Yea, though I walk through the valley of the shadow of death, I will fear no evil, for thou art with me."

"Blessed are the Peacemakers..."

Blessed *indeed* are the soldiers, the sailors, the marines, the airmen and the coast guardsmen who work, fight, and too often die for peace and freedom, "...for they shall be called the children of God."

> Our Heavenly Father, we pause today to remember our fallen brothers and sisters. We honor their supreme sacrifice for the cause of peace and freedom. Our freedom which we too often take for granted. Let us never forget their sacrifice. Be with their families, with whom we share their loss. Be they friends, neighbors, our own families, or even strangers. May their supreme sacrifice—the ultimate price—for all freedom-loving people, not be in vain. May we always, always remember.
>
> Amen.

Memorial Day Sunday Sermon, May 29, 2011
Trinity United Methodist Church
Bowling Green, Ohio
Written and delivered by Herbert Dettmer

Can anyone relate another War Story?

What Makes Me a Christian?

Good things have happened to me, things and deeds I have planned for and worked for. My family, friends, job, home, car, all the material things I possess, I have done what needed to be done to obtain these.

Yes, good things have happened to me, but so have bad things. The puppy we had when I was a boy died. The time I fell and had to go to hospital when I was a little older. My grandparents died, then an uncle. My best friend moved away while we were in high school. My girlfriend dumped me just before homecoming. Later in life, some jerk was promoted before me and let everyone know he was "smarter" than us. (But he really wasn't.)

I try as hard as I can, but things don't always work out the way I plan for them to work. As much as I think I control my life, I am not in control; God is. For I am a sinner and am unworthy of the love that God has for me.

Yet despite or in spite of my unworthiness, God does love me. He loves me so much, He sent His Son, the Savior, to die for my sins. All I have to do is follow Him, learn from His teachings, and seek His forgiveness.

What makes me a Christian? My baptism? My confirmation? God knows I am a sinner. He knows I've broken commandments and don't always follow the golden rule. I've cheated, lied, skipped going to church, had impure thoughts, and so much more, I can't remember. Does this make me a bad Christian? Are there such people as good and bad Christians? So what does it take to be a good Christian? Try as I will, I still sin, and He still forgives. There is no such thing as a good or bad Christian. Either I am a Christian, or I am not. I believe in Christ our Savior, and I am repentant of my sins. God made me, and He made me far from perfect.

So, what makes this *sinner* a Christian?

> I resist temptation—at least most of the time.
>
> I do know right from wrong—even though I don't always do the right thing.
>
> I have learned from my mistakes—and try not to repeat them.
>
> I forgive and forget—well maybe not always forget.
>
> I am humble, following Christ's example—at least I try to be.
>
> I repent of my sins, and ask God's forgiveness—but not always willingly.
>
> I am not perfect; God made this way, but He has shown me the *one* way to live, through His Son, my Savior.
>
> I am a sinner, and God forgives me.
>
> So just *what* does make me a Christian?

The fact that I can and do seek forgiveness of my sins and sincerely try to follow the teachings of Jesus Christ my Savior.

—Herbert Dettmer

What makes *you* a Christian?

January—and Memories of a Christmas Carol

January is "the pits." The Holiday decorations have been taken down and put away. The joyous Christmas carols have been replaced by "normal" music. Sidewalk Santas are pursuing other endeavors.

January is here. The holiday excitement is gone. The skiers are out on the slopes or at least ready to go. Most of us are sitting around complaining about the how much snow we have and how cold it is. The nights are long. The depressing dark of winter is here. Every year it's the same. Christmas and New Years, the height of parties and socializing, celebrating our Savior's birth, then *bam*—the January letdown. Spring is too far away to even think about. Yet "I Heard the Bells on Christmas Day" still echoes in my mind.

Headlines of murders, robberies, car thefts, terror threats, and the economy fill the daily news, adding to the depressing nature of January—dark and dreary. Despair fills us with…wait a minute!…Despair, "I Heard the Bells" says something about that:

> And in despair I bowed my head,
> There is no peace on Earth, I said,
> For hate is strong and mocks the song,

Of peace on Earth, goodwill to men.

Even this beautiful carol talks of the despair and the depression we all feel during post-holiday times. What has our world come to? Violence and hate *have* prevailed. *But wait!* That's not what the carol says. Hate may be strong and often louder than love, but listen carefully to the words.

> Then peeled the bells more loud and deep,
> God is *not* dead, nor doth he sleep.
> The wrong shall fail, the right *prevail*,
> With peace on Earth, goodwill to men.

This isn't our world. As much as we try to think we are in control of it, we aren't. "Our" world belongs to God. He created it and gave us the duty and responsibility to care for it. God is watching, ever watching, and not sleeping. He is watching each one of us. No matter how poorly we may feel, no matter what causes our despair, God is in control. When He decides, and only then, will "the wrong fail and the right prevail."

February—a Lesson in Midwinter

February—midwinter—by now we should be used to the cold and snow. It seems like years ago the last time it was warm outside. Inside, the furnace has kept us warm. It's not hard to think of reasons *not* to go out after dinner. Choosing to stay in curled up with a book or the TV. The kids are restless and always find some reason *not* to do their homework. Slowly, ever so slowly, we notice the sun is setting later each day. Maybe there is hope. Maybe at long last spring will come. Maybe?

Mid-February brings Valentine's Day, a day for love and romance. But why just one day? Why can't we "celebrate" every day with love? There are many kinds of love, and there is more to love than just romance. What did Jesus teach us? To love one another? To love our enemies and pray for those who persecute us? When was the last time any of us did that? If you have to think about it, it's been too long.

February, the month which reminds us of love, with paper hearts, candy hearts, cards, flowers, and dinners out. "Love makes the world go 'round," says the song. How true and yet how sad. How sad there isn't more love in our hearts. Sure, you love your wife or husband and your kids. But what about the stranger you just rushed past? The one you almost bumped into and didn't even say excuse me or smile at? Because you were in too much of a hurry. The Samaritan took care of a stranger when others walked by him. Isn't that love? Jesus taught and still teaches *that* kind of love. We know we should, or have we forgotten? Is it easier to just go on our own way and not be concerned about others? We can write a check to help those in need—Hurricane Katrina and the Lake Township tornados. Is this love? Or is it love when we help with our labors and offer our time and compassion to those suffering from tragedy. Writing a check makes a nice tax deduction, but is it love?

Is it the same love the Samaritan showed on that desolate road so long ago? Have we ever done something similar for someone else, expecting nothing in return? When was the last time we did anything for someone else—anonymously?

February—midwinter—spring is coming—Valentine's Day—love.

When was the last time we showed a stranger or even a friend, what *real* love is all about?

March—the Lion and the Lamb

March is here; the bitter cold of winter is gone. Days are longer, and it isn't dark at dinner time. There is a certain feeling in the air. A warmth, maybe only a hint of warmth, but it's there. We can feel it. March roared in like a lion, or so the story goes. Crocuses peek through what is left of the snow. Buds begin to appear in trees and bushes. The air smells better and Old Man Winter slinks away—to hibernate?

Spring is here. There still may be snow—new snow—maybe even a lot of it, but it won't last. It can't. The world of nature begins to come out of its winter slumber. It is time for a renewal—a rebirth. Flowers will soon bloom, and the grass will grow. We'll turn in our snow shovels and snow blowers for lawn mowers and garden tools. Spring cleaning starts, repairs are made, and people feel, look, and act happier.

March—the beginning of spring, rebirth, renewal, and Lent.

Lent—the season of anticipation. Anticipation and penitence. How many of us really think about Lent? And do something about it? Do we really understand it? How often do we give up something for Lent? Something that we would miss? Or has that tradition been lost? Why do we or did we give up something? The tradition was—is—an act of penitence. The expression of moral anguish we feel for our sins and misdeeds. The anguish we feel or should feel when we beg forgiveness of our sins and misdoings. From Ash Wednesday to Easter morning, how often do we even think about those events which occurred over two thousand years ago? As the world around us begins to grow again, as the lion roars in the new month, as we wait in eager anticipation, let us not just wait. Let's look at ourselves, our lives, and our personal beliefs. Let us look inside our very being. Are we living what we believe? Can we? Should we? Only we know the answer. Can you? And you? And me?

As each of us again experiences the warm air, the spring rain, and maybe even snow, as we watch the buds start growing into leaves and flowers, let us renew ourselves. We've heard the lion roar in early March. When this month closes, maybe we can be like the lamb. Our shepherd will guide us and lead us, then we will truly be "the sheep of His pasture."

April—Triumph and Tragedy and...

April showers cleanse the air, washing away the gloom of winter. The car gets washed, the lawn fertilized, flowers are planted, and the patio furniture is set out.

The first thing we do is try to 'fool' everyone. Sometimes it's even funny. Baseball season starts. Then we rush to make sure our taxes are paid. Eagerly we listen to the triumphant entrance into Jerusalem. Hosanna and Palms. How happy the people were that day. Finally, the Romans would be driven out of Israel. The Jews would be free again. How quickly events changed. Soon only a few followers remained. A dinner, His last. The night in a garden. The arrest and trial, the cross on Calvary. The tomb. His friends abandon Him, even deny knowing Him. How fickle the people were then. How fickle we are today.

Any leader, then and now, must demonstrate—prove—their ability to lead, so the people will follow. Ask any fallen political leader how quickly supporters will vanish because of just one mistake. Did Christ make a mistake? People followed Him, believed in Him, and knew He was the Son of God. But then...

How often tragedy follows triumph. On Palm Sunday, as Jesus rode into the city, throngs of people followed. How quickly they turned against Him. Had

He failed them? They wanted no part of His teachings or of Him. "Crucify Him," they said. Did Jesus fail? Or did the people fail to comprehend what He was saying? Did the people fail to comprehend the prophecy? Have we failed to comprehend what Jesus taught? When will "the meek inherit the Earth?"

On the third day, we know what happened. The greatest triumph of all time. Greater than the entrance into the city. Greater than anything before—or since. Christ conquered death. He died for us, paying for our sins, and arose from the dead. We call it— the Resurrection.

Every year we hear the story of Easter, but do we truly understand it? The symbolism of the lamb and the lion is not just for the month of March. Do we fully understand the significance of the Lamb, the humility Jesus taught? Do we understand what He did for us? Of course we do. Don't we?

May—
and a Mother Wept

The month of May brings us warm, fresh, clean air. School is almost over. We hear lawn mowers, children playing, our neighbor's stereo. The dandelions are in full bloom, birds sing…and a mother wept.

Little children work hard to make their mothers that special present for *her* day, older children too. Fathers take their wives and mothers out to dinner, give them flowers or a corsage…and a mother wept.

A mother wept at her son's grave. She remembered that day, so long ago, the day she learned her son was dead, killed on some distant shore. He was a good boy, honest and sincere. He wanted to be a minister. But first he answered a different call, a much different call. Freedom was challenged, then threatened, then attacked! Freedom had to be defended! Freedom was not—is not—free. It must be paid for with pain, suffering, and sometimes blood...and a mother wept, many mothers, fathers too.

Through two World Wars, Korea, Vietnam, Desert Storm, Afghanistan, and Iraq, all through our nation's history... mothers have wept. On distant shores, in foreign lands, sons, and daughters too, have laid down their lives for the cause of freedom. At home we hear the words sacrifice, bravery, honor. In the Holy Bible in the Gospel of John we read these words, "Greater love has no man than this; that he lay down his life for his friends." ...and a mother wept.

People gather in cemeteries, churches, and public parks as they have since 1867. Flags fly at half-staff honoring those who have fallen, whose supreme sacrifice we remember each year. Side-by-side stand an attorney, a factory worker, a business manager, an unskilled laborer, joined by a common bond. A wreath is placed at the memorial. Each man—veterans—stand shoulder-to-shoulder, a tear perhaps more than one, leaks out of their eyes...*they* remember. The honor guard fires a volley of shots...and a mother wept.

The flag is raised to full staff, flapping proudly in the breeze. *Freedom lives!* Defended by those who served, who fought, who died.

"Greater love has no man than this..." ...and a mother wept.

Let us remember as we cut the grass, watch children play, and enjoy a barbeque in the warm, fresh, clean air of May, it might have been different, very different.

Let us never forget those who *bought* the freedom we enjoy today with their supreme sacrifice. And let us be comforted knowing, they are with God, our Father, in Heaven.

"Greater love... " and a mother wept.

"May...and a Mother Wept" was written as a tribute to Herbert Fish, who gave his life on Okinawa in April of 1945. His mother, Ethel Fish, gave me the notebook he took overseas, from which many of the prayers and verses in this collection come. Some are his own writings, and some he copied from various sources, which are unknown to me. At this writing I have added Afghanistan and Iraq. Not all wars and military actions have been mentioned, but all through our nation's history, Americans—men and women, rich and poor, from all ethnic, racial, and religious backgrounds—have given their lives for our freedom. This tribute was written for Herbert Fish and *all* who have died for our country.

—hd

June—at Last!

June—school is out! Graduations, vacations, warm—
no hot weather is here! Swimming, golfing, boating,
fishing. The days are long and evenings offer soft,
pleasant breezes. People take long walks in the park or
maybe just around the block. Flowers bloom, birds are
singing, and squirrels frolic.

We stop and to give our fathers something special
just for him, for *his* day. On another day we honor the
flag of our great country.

It's summer; no longer are we cooped up inside,
trapped. Winter coats, gloves, and boots have been put
away, replaced by shorts, T-shirts, and bathing suits.
Our feet are often bare.

Vacations take us to dreamed of locations for fun
and relaxation. People smile and laugh, tend to their
flowers and gardens, go on picnics and barbeques. It
may rain or even storm, but nothing can take away the
joy and warmth of summer.

While we are enjoying ourselves with the newness of
summer, how often do we forget the miracles of nature,
of life, which bring us out of winter, through spring,
and into summer? How many of us "skip" church dur-
ing these warm, pleasant days. Is it less important to
worship God then? Or just less convenient? Between
golf, boating, ball games, all-day picnics, and other
activities there doesn't seem to be time to go to church.

Maybe we say, "It was a long, hard winter; we need to enjoy ourselves." Some kind of rationalization like that to ease our minds.

Then when trouble strikes, or illness, or injury, we quickly turn to God to make everything right. And does God listen? Of course He does. Does God answer our prayers? Certainly, not always in the way we want, but He does answer. Could this be a test of our Faith? Could it be God's way of reminding us that He loves us? That we are still His children? That whether we worship Him in church or outside or not at all, He is always there.

He is always there for us, no matter what. Shouldn't we pay more attention to Him? Shouldn't we "be there" for Him? Or have we become so self-reliant and independent we can take care of ourselves? If so, then why do we so quickly turn to God when things don't go the way we want them to? Have we become so self-reliant and independent that we have forgotten the lessons of humility that Jesus taught us?

The answer is inside each of us. It should be easy. While we enjoy the warm summer weather of June, let us take the time and make the effort to remember whose world we live in.

July—Fireworks, Swimming, Baseball, and Picnics

July—days at the beach or pool, or maybe on the boat. The summer we've been looking forward to is here, in full force—backyard BBQs, a parade, and fireworks to celebrate Independence Day. Forgotten are the cold, snowy days of winter. Forgotten as well are the struggles and sacrifices made by those who built our great nation. Time to remember those sacrifices and the blessings we have living in this great nation.

As we enjoy the warm—even hot—summer days of July, at a baseball game or family vacation, let us remember hot weather often brings thunder storms and severe storms. Take cover when storms threaten, and pray for safety. While praying let us think about the beauty of nature as well as the power of nature. The beauty of a warm summer day, with flowers blooming, trees full of green leaves, small puffy white clouds floating by. But we must also be aware of the force of severe thunderstorms, winds, and what tornados can and will do.

Nature is a marvelous force; we can enjoy a walk in the woods beside a slowly moving stream with a gentle breeze blowing. It is also powerful force we cannot control. Hurricanes, earthquakes, tornados, blizzards, floods, and droughts strike every year somewhere on earth. As much as we think we are in control of our lives, we must remember, nature will always have the last word. That word may be good or bad, but nature will always win. Even though we may pollute the air and water, in time nature will fix it. Maybe not in our time or to our liking, but nature was here before mankind was here and will be here after mankind is gone.

As we enjoy the warm—maybe hot—days of July, let us all stop and appreciate all the good nature has provided for us. Picnics and baseball games often get rained out, that is just a small disappointment compared to what nature can do. Let us thank our creator for all the wonders of nature.

August—It's Still Hot, and School Starts

Hot August days and warm nights. This might be your vacation month. The long-awaited time to visit friends or family who live far away. But the grass still needs to be mowed and the flowers still need attention. School starts soon, and plans begin for the fall season. But not quite yet! It's still summer!

The bright, hot, sometimes stormy days are not over. There is still time to catch another baseball game or to realize how beautiful our home and yard is. We might think back briefly to the blizzard earlier this year—just briefly. We gaze at the wonders of nature and admire all of God's handiwork. Now the trees are full of green leaves; our gardens and the farmer's fields are nearly ready for harvest. We think back to last winter when everything was so stark and bare and cold. What a difference!

How can there be such a contrast? What could have made such beauty and warmth? Could that same "what" make such a stark, barren, and cold landscape as well? For reasons we will never know, God, our creator, did. Our scientists and weather forecasters will explain the reasons as they understand all the factors they study. But the *real* reason is unknown to us. Just as we don't understand why a loving creator "allows" earthquakes, hurricanes, and tornados to destroy part of His creation from time to time. We can only guess and speculate. Why would a loving creator "allow" all the damage and destruction, all the hate and sinful living we see?

Could it be that He "allows" this to see how we act and react to these negatives? And what, if anything, we do about it? Is our life here on earth a test? To see how we handle the challenges of living with each other? How we handle the challenges of nature? Are we Good Samaritans? Do we turn the other cheek? Do we go the extra mile? Do we follow the Ten Commandments and the Golden Rule?

As we continue to enjoy our summer, our vacations, start to get ready for school and the fall season, let us take a moment, maybe two (or even three), to reflect on how we are living. Are we living up to our "potential"? Are we really living the life we know we should be living? God gave us a beautiful home—earth—and the rules to live by. Are we living the way we know we should? Are we passing the test?

September—School, Football, and Fall Begins

September, the kids are back in school, days are shorter, and sometimes one can feel a certain crispness in the air, especially at night. But it still can be hot, sometimes very hot. The "dog days of summer" are here, and with them—football. Baseball teams are closing in on the playoffs, and the leaves are just starting to turn. Vacations are remembered. We remember, with grief, the events of September 11, 2001. Fall activities begin. Summer "ends" as we celebrate Labor Day with picnics, parades, and rallies. The farmers get ready to harvest their crops, hoping the market will be in their favor.

Those who ski look forward to the coming snow and ski slopes, while others look forward to the first frost, which will help their allergies. Another season begins, another change in God's world. Some birds start to fly south for the coming winter and hibernating animals begin to settle down for their winter's nap. The world of nature is tired and prepares itself for a well earned rest. The world of nature, God's world, is beginning another part of its never-ending cycle.

Do we ever think of the wonders of nature? How well nature works when left alone? The strong survive, and the weak perish. Strong trees bend to the wind and storms, and strong animals seek shelter. While the weak trees fall and weak animals die, life goes on, and nature, as always, is able to rebound. Not always as soon we would like, but then again, it's not our world we live in, it is God's. No matter how hard we try to stand up to nature, with our houses, buildings, and other man-made structures, nature always seems to prevail. If we've taken shortcuts to save money and a storm hits, those weak structures suffer, as do those who occupy them. The laws of nature, the laws of physics, can't be violated. The same is true for the law of gravity. These laws are really the laws of God, for who or what else is nature?

Just as the laws of nature can't be violated, neither can other laws of God be violated. What is the difference between God and nature? Or is God nature? What about those shortcuts we've taken to save money and time? Have we always done our jobs as well as we can and know we should? Aren't these shortcuts, "cheating"? Those little lies and fabrications we tell to look good or save us from embarrassment, aren't they, "Bearing false witness"? Think about it.

As we begin another season, let us all look carefully at our lives. While we watch our football and baseball teams win or loose, and our kids start another school year, are we obeying all the laws of nature? Are we obeying the laws of God?

October—Changing Leaves, Halloween, and Life's Test

Fall schedules are well established, trees change to spectacular colors, there is a definite crispness in the air, especially in the morning. Winter coats, gloves, mittens, and even boots are brought out for the coming of snow. Our gardens are prepared for winter, and the grass is cut, probably for the last time.

The seasons are changing again. Nature prepares for a long winters rest, yet our schedules get busier. With homecoming activities, Halloween is coming, then the Christmas season approaches. As we settle into the fall season with school, community, and church activities (the World Series and football), let us not become so involved we lose sight of what is really important. The world of nature slows down for a reason. Our creator designed the seasons to give life a cycle. Dormant winter gives into the rebirth of spring. Summer is for producing crops (food) and autumn is the time for harvest.

As we settle into our busy fall schedule there is never enough time to do everything. Is there ever enough time for reflection? Reflection about why we are here. Why did God create us and put us on earth? Why did God give us so many problems and challenges? The garden of Eden was perfect, except for the Tree of Knowledge.

Could our life here on earth be a test? Is it a test to see how we act and react to life's challenges?

When everything is "under control," and we are healthy and happy, how do we act? Do we strut around, brag, and maybe even show off? Has our success become the purpose of our lives? What ever happened to the lesson of humility? Do we understand what Christ was teaching us when He washed His disciples' feet? Is service to others for someone else?

When life gives us a serious challenge—a job loss or health problems—how do we handle that? Do we deal with it as best we can? Or do we whine and cry about how life is so unfair to us? Do we make excuses or try to blame someone else for our troubles? When we are wronged, do we forgive and forget? (Or at least forgive.)

October—the change of seasons—a busy time for all of us. A time when there is too little time for reflection. A time when we could be failing the test of life, or are we passing?

November—Election Day, Colder Weather, and Thanksgiving

November starts with the end of the fall campaign and Election Day. Those wonderful or annoying campaign ads and flyers are all but over. Colder temperatures, with rain or even snow tell us that winter is close at hand. Skiers are delighted as are the snowman (and snowwoman) builders. We take a day to honor our military veterans, for without them and their service, just where would we be? Schools begin preparing for winter programs, as the holidays as fast approaching.

The busiest of seasons, with all the traditions, joys, and memories. We think of all our blessings and our families and friends. Remembering those who have passed on, we continue to live and work and try to comprehend what it must have been like that first Thanksgiving. After a bitterly cold and harsh first year, then the growing season and harvest. How the Pilgrims and natives were able to come together and share in the bounty of the harvest.

How different it is today with all the problems we face and the divisions in our society. Yet the Pilgrims faced even more problems, more serious problems. Their very existence was in doubt during their first year in the new world. But they worked hard and probably complained about the reality of what they faced. They complained, but they worked, sacrificed, and survived. Working with the natives they reaped a bountiful harvest and prepared the first Thanksgiving dinner.

How easy it would have been to give up during that harsh first year. But with their faith in God and their faith in each other they made it and prospered. How often do we complain about how "bad" it is for us, of the numerous problems we face every day, our annoying neighbors, perhaps our coworkers, or maybe that jerk in front of us in traffic. Do we really have it that bad? Think about the Pilgrims on that first Thanksgiving Day and the problems they faced. Could we have survived and overcome their problems?

As we give thanks this month, think about our Pilgrim forefathers as we eat our dinner. Remember them as we watch our football games, feeling a little too full. Remember them as we start the holiday season. Our problems pale in comparison to theirs. We are here today because of them.

December—Winter Arrives, Shopping, and Christmas

December—the holidays are upon us, and winter. We begin with Advent—the anticipation of the birth of our Savoir. Then we remember that fateful morning in Hawaii at Pearl Harbor—a day that will live in infamy, a day that changed our nation. As we begin the holiday season, the shopping, decorating, gift wrapping and remembering family traditions, are we so caught up in the preparations we forget the true meaning of the birth of our Savior? Christmas programs at school and church by our children, community holiday concerts, the parties, and Christmas cards and letters for all our friends.

Have we forgotten the *significance* of Christ's birth in a *humble* stable? Have we forgotten that Christ taught us about love and humility? With all our worldly possessions and busy schedules do we even have time to think about what God's gift to us means? A Savior, to teach us, to guide our lives, and eventually to die for us. But we are too busy with careers, community activities, and our families and friends to give any real thought to what really happened in that stable so long ago. We go through the motions, we do what is expected, and we buy so many things we can't really afford. We try to do the right thing, but Santa Claus, his elves, and his reindeer always seem first and foremost in our minds.

The tiny baby in the manger, with the shepherds, the wise men, and Mary and Joseph is *the* Christmas story. Yet we are told the December holiday is a "Winter Holiday." (We don't want to "offend" anyone, by calling it *Christmas*.) We are also told the December holiday has its roots in a pagan feast. Everyone—some who are not even Christians—is telling us how to celebrate the birth of our Savior. How we can't display religious Christmas decorations on public property and we can't even say "Christmas" in our schools. Christ is in our hearts and in our homes. We should celebrate *our* holiday, the birth of our Savior, as intended by our Heavenly Father, and spread the good news to whoever is willing to listen.

The Christmas Holiday is about the birth of Jesus and the celebration of God's gift to us, which is symbolized by the exchanging of gifts. Let us keep the *true* meaning of Christmas in our hearts and minds and in our communities.

Final Thoughts

Why are there so many different "interpretations" to Biblical verses and stories? How do they affect our faith and our belief? Or do they? Do we "interpret" God's Word to justify our own selfish needs and desires?

Think about God's gift of the earth to us, how many of us take the gift and try to save it for, perhaps eternity. It honors the Giver when we use and enjoy the gift, rather than saving it, almost as if we didn't want the offering.